SEXUAL ISSUES IN FAMILY THERAPY

James C. Hansen, Editor
Jane Divita Woody
Robert Henley Woody, Volume Editors

The Family Therapy Collections

AN ASPEN PUBLICATION ®

Aspen Systems Corporation
Rockville, Maryland
London
1983

Library of Congress Cataloging in Publication Data
Main entry under title:

Sexual issues in family therapy.

(The family therapy collections, ISSN 0735-9152)
Includes bibliographies.
1. Family psychotherapy. 2. Sex (Psychology)
3. Sexual disorders. I. Hansen, James C.
II. Woody, Jane Divita III. Woody, Robert Henley
IV. Series.
RC488.5.S48   1983   616.89'156   83-2551
ISBN: 0-89443-605-8

Publisher: John Marozsan
Managing Editor: Margot Raphael
Printing and Manufacturing: Debbie Collins

Library of Congress Catalog Card Number: 81-20677
ISBN: 0-89443-605-8
ISSN: 0735-9152

Printed in the United States of America

1   2   3   4   5

Table of Contents

Board of Editors

Contributors

Volume Editors

JANE DIVITA WOODY
AND
ROBERT HENLEY WOODY

KAREN AUTHIER
University of Nebraska at Omaha
College of Medicine
Nebraska Psychiatric Institute
Omaha, Nebraska

JULIE G. BOTVIN-MADORSKY
Casa Colina Hospital
Pomona, California

DIANE B. BRASHEAR
Brashear Center, Inc.
Indiana University School of
Social Work
Indianapolis, Indiana

COLLIER M. COLE
The University of Texas Medical
Branch at Galveston
School of Allied Health Science
Galveston, Texas

LESLIE E. COLLINS
Creighton University
School of Medicine
Omaha, Nebraska

JOHN L. EBLING
Metro Health Plan
Brashear Center, Inc.
Indianapolis, Indiana

JAMES W. MADDOCK
Meta Resources
St. Paul, Minnesota

CANDACE WARD-MCKINLAY
Casa Colina Hospital
Pomona, California

THOMAS WARD-MCKINLAY
Casa Colina Hospital
Pomona, California

JANE DIVITA WOODY
School of Social Work
University of Nebraska at Omaha
Omaha, Nebraska

ROBERT HENLEY WOODY
University of Nebraska at Omaha
Omaha, Nebraska

NATHALIA ZIMMERMAN
Creighton University
School of Medicine
Omaha, Nebraska

Preface

The Family Therapy Collections is a series of publications reviewing topics of current and specific interest and translating theory and research into practical applications. Each volume serves as a source of information for the practicing professional by synthesizing and applying the literature of the field. Each *Collection* contains articles, authored by practicing professionals, that provide in-depth coverage of a single aspect of family therapy.

Family therapy frequently requires dealing with sexual issues. A sexual issue may be the presenting problem or it may emerge as part of another concern. This *Collection* provides therapists with information about sexual issues and methods to use the information in appropriate interventions.

A family therapist is in a unique position to work with sexual problems. Indeed, sexuality can be seen to be the basis of all family interaction. The therapist can help resolve relations between spouses that could affect other family dynamics. The therapist can also help parents discuss information with a child, explore attitudes about sex, or work through behaviors that violate family or social restrictions. Sexual issues certainly affect family members and acceptance and resolution with the most significant people is a crucial concern.

The therapist uses knowledge of the dynamics of the sexual issue and the understanding of family dynamics as a basis for a relevant intervention. It is imperative that a therapist have knowledge not only of family therapy but also of sexuality. Many family therapists have not received specific training in sex therapy but with appropriate information can use their skills to assist families in resolving a specific issue. In situations requiring more specific treatment, referral to a trained sex therapist may be needed. As therapists encounter or uncover sexual issues, there is a need for diagnostic and therapeutic skills to provide relevant intervention approaches.

Jane Divita Woody, PhD, MSW, and Robert Henley Woody, PhD, ScD, JD, are co-editors of *Sexual Issues in Family Therapy*. Dr. Jane Woody, the senior editor, is an associate professor of social work at the University of Nebraska at Omaha and the coordinator for the School of Social Work's new specialization in the area of marriage and family therapy. She teaches courses in sexual issues and sex therapy and therapeutic approaches to marriage, divorce, and remarriage adjustment. She has authored numerous publications in sexuality, divorce, and family therapy. In addition, she maintains a part-time private practice. Dr. Robert Woody is professor of psychology at the University of Nebraska at Omaha and teaches courses in clinical assessment and psychology and the law. He is involved in supervision and research in marriage, sex, and family therapies and maintains private practices in law and in clinical/forensic psychology. He is an approved supervisor for the American Association for Marriage and Family Therapy, and he is chairman of the AAMFT Judicial Council. He is the author/editor of 13 books and over 200 articles for professional journals. Both editors are certified as sex therapists and sex educators by the American Association for Sex Educators, Counselors, and Therapists. They have selected outstanding authors to write articles that cover a range of sexual issues. This volume as a whole provides therapists with information that will assist them well in understanding and intervening in sexual issues they will encounter in family therapy.

James C. Hansen
Editor
February, 1983

Introduction

It takes only a Saturday night of family television to confirm the widely heralded presence of the sexual revolution. To be sure, few would doubt that the brave new world has arrived, and, like Huxley's novel, it is receiving diverse reviews. For over two decades, dramatic and continuous changes in sexual attitudes, values, and behavior have emerged in all aspects of society. Individuals as well as social institutions (such as the legal system, church, and family) have had to confront and deal with these changes. Perhaps most disturbing for many people has been the concern about the impact of the new sexuality on family life.

Maintaining a reasonably harmonious and stable family life has always been difficult, but the complexities and hazards of modern society make it seem an even more arduous task today. At the same time, many facets of contemporary society support and enrich family life as never before. The sexual revolution appears to be one of those facets that has contributed to both positive and negative outcomes.

Consider for the moment only one part of the phenomenon, the extensive media attention that has removed much of the taboo labeling previously applied to sex topics. For some individuals and families, the availability of new information has been used in a way to enhance their lives. For others, however, it has contributed to conflicts and problems, many of which are encountered in therapy.

On the positive side, the greater openness toward and specific focus on sexuality has enabled some persons, independently and without professional help, to acknowledge and accept their own sexuality as an integral part of their existence. Consequently, with increased knowledge and comfort, they can discuss sex with those persons most intimately involved with them—partners, spouses, children, and friends. Many women, especially, have become more able to affirm their sexual needs and to seek their fulfillment.

But not all of the media efforts regarding sexuality have been positive, nor has the information necessarily been used in a positive way. Stereotyped or unrealistic sexual identities abound for the individual either to emulate or to use as a comparative reference. For example, an attractive 30-year-old married female client experiencing no sexual desire decided that she was not sexual because she did not measure up to the typical *Playboy* centerfold. Another negative outcome has been the compartmentalization of sex as an independent function; clients often expect their sexual organs to perform for all occasions, regardless of whether the behavior is congruent with their identities, beliefs, or values. Finally, some persons have seized upon sexual technique, performance, and image as primarily narcissistic goals to the exclusion of interpersonal factors such as caring, regard, loving, and commitment.

Family therapists today face more and more clients experiencing anxieties, conflicts, and problem behaviors in the sexual area. The increase in this type of clinical situation is probably due to the societal change that has given people permission to acknowledge and deal with such problems. Do clinicians have the specialized knowledge necessary for helping such clients? This volume represents an effort to address this question.

The impetus to evolve new ways of assessing and treating sexual problems was primarily generated by Masters and Johnson (1966, 1970), whose major contribution was the joint focus on the dyad and on the current manifestation of dysfunction as the key to therapeutic change. Additional elaborations and refinements of their milestone achievement have subsequently enriched the whole field of sex education and therapy (Kaplan, 1974, 1979). It is, therefore, important to acknowledge the contribution of diverse theoretical approaches to this expanding and eclectic field of practice.

We are grateful to the authors who have tapped their expertise and structured it into concise articles. Their contributions increase understanding and clarity about the impact of sexuality on the individual's and family's overall sense of well-being. Each of the articles is critical with respect to the broad goals of this volume, which are to (1) sensitize therapists to the pervasiveness of sexual issues in family function and dysfunction; (2) increase knowledge of selected major sex-related concerns of clients; and (3) posit specific practice guidelines and techniques that are readily integrated into the key approaches to marriage and family therapy.

The authors are all experienced practitioners and specialists, not only in sex counseling but also in marriage and family therapy; in addition, they function as educators and supervisors in these areas. They appreciate the fact that client sexual concerns often surface in the context of other problems being addressed in therapy, and they believe that many such problems can be dealt with competently by the original therapist without the need for referral. Their contributions are aimed at increasing that level of competence.

Included in *Sexual Issues in Family Therapy* are articles that discuss the most common and distressing types of sexual concerns. The authors carefully delineate the sexual issues involved and draw upon other sources as well as their own clinical expertise to outline effective therapeutic principles. In an introductory overview, Dr. James Maddock addresses the important conceptual issue of integrating knowledge of human sexuality with critical concepts from family systems theory, psychodynamic psychology, and individual and family life cycle perspectives. Dr. Diane Brashear and Mr. John Ebling focus on the crucial interface between genitality and reproductivity and the impact of the decisions required by this interface throughout the life cycle. A cognitive/educational approach is presented by Dr. Collier Cole as an initial strategy suitable for treatment of sexual dysfunctions that emerge in the course of other therapy concerns. The article on sexuality in divorce and remarriage by Dr. Jane Woody emphasizes the adaptations required for the individual and family sexual selves in the face of these crisis situations; suggested therapeutic efforts stress an eclectic approach involving crisis techniques, promotion of insight, and cognitive/behavioral methods that can be applied in both individual and family formats.

The next three articles deal with aspects of sexuality in which professional understanding and knowledge have rapidly expanded in recent years. The authors identify critical information and sources and elaborate on treatment principles designed to assist clients with these complex issues. Dr. Leslie Collins and Ms. Nathalia Zimmerman see the emergence of homosexual and bisexual factors as often impinging on basic family structures and dynamics; hence, they outline therapeutic issues and tasks based on family systems theory. Ms. Karen Authier discusses the many facets and controversial views involved in problems of sexual violence and incest. An eclectic approach is suggested because client outcomes and problems are diverse, for example, assaults on self-integrity, disturbance of interpersonal relationships, imminent family crisis and possible dissolution, and vestiges of these situations that may have an impact on the client years after the actual experience. Drs. Thomas Ward-McKinlay, Candace Ward-McKinlay, and Julie Botvin-Madorsky focus attention on the sexual needs and problems of ill and disabled clients. They present information concerning the effects of major health problems and their treatment on the individual's self-image, sexuality, and interpersonal and family relationships, and they offer specific techniques for dealing openly and sensitively with these problems in the context of both inpatient and outpatient settings. In the final chapter, Dr. Robert Woody acknowledges the possibility of deleterious effects from clinical ineptness with sex problems, offers a frame of reference that accommodates ethical treatment of sexual concerns, and explores the legal implications of sex-related therapies, such as potential malpractice actions.

Beyond didactic knowledge, such as is offered in this volume, effective therapy for sex problems presupposes the therapist's attainment of a certain personal and professional integration. Specifically, the clinician should have internalized the following attitudes: (1) to be sensitive to the special vulnerabilities of clients with sex problems; (2) to be "relatively conflict-free about his or her own sexuality"; (3) to be able to view sexuality as a positive, life-enhancing force; and (4) to be mature and unbiased in regard to gender role differences in love and sex (Kaplan, 1977, p. 185). The integration of such attitudes is achieved primarily through the experiential contexts of careful supervision and training that permit exploration of sexual attitudes and dialogue with others representing divergent views and values. Responsibility remains, therefore, with the individual therapist to assess his or her overall knowledge about sexuality along with experiential readiness to work with sex problems.

REFERENCES

Kaplan, H.S. *The new sex therapy.* New York: Brunner/Mazel, 1974.

Kaplan, H.S. *Disorders of sexual desire.* New York: Brunner/Mazel, 1979.

Kaplan, H.D. Training of sex therapists. In W.M. Masters, V.E. Johnson, & R.C. Kolodny (Eds.), *Ethical issues in sex therapy and research.* Boston: Little, Brown, 1977.

Masters, W.H., & Johnson, V.E. *Human sexual response.* Boston: Little, Brown, 1966.

Masters, W.H., & Johnson, V.E. *Human sexual inadequacy.* Boston: Little, Brown, 1970.

Jane Divita Woody
Robert Henley Woody
Volume Editors
February, 1983

1. Human Sexuality in the Life Cycle of the Family System

James W. Maddock, PhD
META Resources, PA
St. Paul, Minnesota

School of Public Health
Department of Family Social Sciences
University of Minnesota
Minneapolis, Minnesota

ASSOCIATING THE TERMS "HUMAN SEXUALITY" AND "FAMILY system" has a variety of implications, depending upon the context in which they are juxtaposed. To some, the terms seem to have little in common; to others, they suggest matters that are deeply interrelated. Freud may have exaggerated when he emphasized the pervasive erotic atmosphere of the family as the single most powerful factor in childhood socialization. Nevertheless, in the past two decades research findings have produced renewed appreciation for the immense influence of sex-related phenomena on the individual and collective behavior of family members.

Although Masters and Johnson (1970) founded sex therapy on the systemic principle "Sexual dysfunction is a marital unit problem," the "new sex therapy" (Kaplan, 1974) has nevertheless been elaborated largely by researchers and clinicians grounded in neobehaviorism and related individualistic frameworks (Annon, 1975; LoPiccolo & LoPiccolo, 1978). Widely used by therapists treating marital and family problems, brief sex therapy has not been conceptually related to emerging family systems theory. To be sure, investigating human sexuality in the family brings one face to face with the dilemma of linking concepts from family systems theory with those of psychodynamic psychology, and of interlocking principles from individual life cycle development (primarily psychological) with those of the family life cycle (mainly sociological). Equally as formidable is the challenge of devising a comprehensive theoretical basis for marital, sex, and family therapies.

However, some developments in the past decade suggest that it may soon be possible to advance a theory of the life cycle of the family system that could serve also as a framework for family therapy. For example, the individual life cycle framework brilliantly initiated by Erik Erikson (1950, 1959) has been refined and elaborated by other writers (Gould, 1978; Levinson, 1978; Neugarten, 1968). Similarly, sociological thinking about the family life cycle has been enriched by concepts and principles drawn from psychology and social psychology, fostering partial integration of individual life cycle and family life cycle perspectives (Hill, 1970; Rodgers, 1962). More recently, family life cycle and family systems concepts have begun to be explored and interlocked (Carter & McGoldrick, 1980). At the same time, systems thinking has produced a "second generation" of family therapists whose ways of working with family behavior and change are evolving a new "systems therapy " (Hoffman, 1981). With the publication in 1973 of *Uncommon Therapy*, Jay Haley's book on the work of Milton Erickson, the relationship of family therapy techniques to the family life cycle began to be explicitly explored. Since that time, the clinical and

2

theoretical work of structural and strategic therapists has skillfully elaborated the relationship between family problems, individual symptoms, and the transitions between stages of the family life cycle (Haley, 1980; Minuchin, Rosman & Baker, 1978). But perhaps most important of all are the serious efforts now under way to advance integrative paradigms linking family systems concepts with those of both the individual life cycle and the family life cycle (Terkelson, 1980).

Coincidental with these developments in family theory and therapy have been several important advances in thinking about human sexuality. First of all, changes in social attitudes toward sexual behavior and, in particular, toward the scientific study of sex have permitted a rather dramatic increase in sexual knowledge, among both professionals and the public at large. Research data on human sexual behavior has come to be largely organized around developmental and life cycle principles (Gadpaille, 1975; Money, 1980). Further, conceptualizations of sexual behavior have increasingly reflected an interactional rather than an individualistic perspective (Money & Ehrhardt, 1972; Petras, 1980). And, of course, there have been substantial improvements in the scope and sophistication of the sex-related therapies referred to above.

Despite these integrative trends, little effort has been made to elaborate the conceptual connections between family theories and theories of sexual behavior. Sex continues to be treated as a special area, both theoretically and clinically, within the family field. The major premise of this article is that sexuality is a primary component of the family system and a fundamental aspect of life inside the family. What follows is an attempt to outline, in at least a preliminary fashion, a model of human sexuality within the context of family life. Certain theoretical constructs will be presented, from which will be derived some conclusions about the characteristics of the   sexually healthy'' family and the underlying dynamics of family ''sexual dis-ease.'' Finally, we will present illustrations of some important sexual issues at various stages of the family life cycle.

THE DIMENSIONS OF FAMILY LIFE

To conceptualize family experience, one must begin with certain basic givens, or existential dimensions. These are the irreducible realities that underlie human experience, what some philosophers have termed ''expressions of being'' in human life (Tillich, 1963). The term ''dimension'' has been deliberately chosen, in part to convey the notion of intersection without interference among the multiple realities of family experience, which are all related in a complex, meaningful way. There are four primary existential dimensions underlying family life: the systemic, the developmental, the sexual, and the historical. (How one characterizes what underlies, or grounds, these existential dimensions will not be addressed here. Ultimately, it is a matter of religious/philosophical belief, involving moral values and statements of faith.)

Systemic

The systemic dimension is the unifying, or organizing, principle of human interaction, and thus of family life. A family system is composed of interdependent parts (members) functioning as a "balanced" unit. As social systems, families have certain properties that define how their members relate. Properties widely agreed to be most important to the family clinician are organizational complexity (including hierarchies and boundaries), openness to interaction with the environment, cohesiveness, information processing capability (circularity and feedback), and stability and adaptability (morphostatic and morphogenic capacities) (Andolfi, 1979; Buckley, 1968; Hoffman, 1981; Kantor & Lehr, 1975; and Olson, Russell, & Sprenkle, 1979).

Developmental

The developmental dimension reflects movement in the human life span—from little to big, from young to old, from birth to death. The life cycle reveals patterns of human experience over time, called "stages," which meaningfully organize discrete variables such as physical size, biological maturation, reproductive capacity, extent and type of social recognition, and so on. Each stage of life calls upon the resources of the individual to accomplish certain "developmental tasks" necessary to the survival and enhancement of that individual as a person and as a member of a social community (Erikson, 1950).

Families, too, move through a life span with successive stages and nodal events linked to the actions of various family members, particularly to their entrances and exits and to transitions in the roles their individual developmental stages permit them to play. At any given point in time, family members are at different stages in their own life cycles, thereby creating a generational hierarchy as well as a complex structure of interlocking perceptions, emotions, relationships, and problems resulting from the "cogwheeling" of their developmental tasks (Duvall, 1962; Erikson, 1950).

Sexual

The sexual dimension of human life is the reality of reproductive "dimorphism" (Money & Ehrhardt, 1972), that is, biological femaleness and maleness expressed as two modes of being-in-the-world. This dimension has two equally important components, which can be conceptually distinguished, though not actually separated. The first is the gender/role component: the expression of a male or female sense of self through certain psychosocial behaviors. The second component is the erotic: the pleasure-seeking orientation of the "embodied" person (Nelson, 1978) of either gender.

The combination of gender complementarity and erotic interest provides one of the basic motivations for the formation and maintenance of a family unit. The family organizes and transmits messages confirming gender identity and outlining acceptable sex role behaviors for both adult and child members. At the same time, through physical and emotional interaction, elements of eroticism pervade the family atmosphere, encouraging the meeting of physical, psychological, and practical needs.

Historical

The historical dimension of life—that is, the intersection of the coordinates of space and time—relates all human experiences in a meaningful context. History gives individuals a sense of continuity with one another—of community—despite experiential differences. History is the environment of the family system. The coordinates of space and time affect a variety of factors, which, in turn, influence both the practical aspects of family life and the meaning of family experiences to members. Most prominent among these relative factors are physical resources, social role expectations, and cultural values.

Perhaps even more important, however, is the fact that the historical dimension of life actualizes the reality of chance occurrences that may deeply affect family members and the family as a whole. Participating in history challenges the family to make shared meanings out of seemingly random events and ambiguous, unpredictable situations. To some of these events, the family will respond using its existing resources, its present organizational structure, and the processes of interaction already learned; that is "first-order change." To other events, the family must respond with "second-order change," in which restructuring of existing organizational patterns occurs. This, in turn, leads to the learning of new interactional processes and, frequently, to the utilization of additional resources not heretofore available to the family, or to particular members (Watzlawick, Weakland, & Fisch, 1974).

THEORETICAL PROPOSITIONS

Understanding the multidimensionality of family life requires the use of a variety of conceptual frameworks, or "existential perspectives" (Edel, 1955). Following is a series of theoretical propositions about family sexuality that presumes the family's multidimensional unity—the intersection of the sexual dimension with the systemic, developmental, and historical dimensions in such a way that the family's experience contains and integrates elements from each of these dimensions into its everyday life.

Proposition 1: Family sexual experience is pervasive and functional rather than isolated and aberrant.

One of the primary motivations for family formation is sexual—a combination of gender complementarity in pair bonding (largely, though not exclusively, predicated upon sexual dimorphism) and an interest in consistent opportunity for erotic expression. Once formed, the family system is undergirded by eroticism (in the broadest sense), which motivates family members to meet each other's needs on a more or less consistent basis. Physical proximity, touch, and exchange of affection are major channels through which family members relate to each other, thereby contributing both to the psychosocial development of individuals and to the stability of the family system as a whole.

Family members share sexual meanings as a powerful way of influencing each other's behavior. Though sexual behavior is largely predicated on its meaning to the behaving individual, behavior acquires full meaning only by its function (actual or symbolic) in an interactional system (Henley, 1977). Any sexual behavior—even solitary activity such as masturbation—can be said to have "message value" vis-à-vis other family members, and thereby to be functional within the family system. (Of course, it may simultaneously have message and function value outside the family system.)

Proposition 2: Since the family unit consists of sexual persons, it represents the social meanings of femaleness and maleness to its members.

Each family must convey to its members information about the sex role expectations they will encounter in their social milieu; conversely, the family is responsible to its social environment for the conformity of its members to these standards. This accountability is felt and expressed in a variety of ways within the family, beginning perhaps in the parents' response to the inevitable question "What is it?" when announcing the birth of a new baby.

Gender identity (the inner sense of "who I am" sexually) and accompanying social behaviors arise out of the complex interaction of a biogenetically coded "program" within the individual and a series of interpersonal developmental events in which sex role expectations are represented to that individual—at first primarily by the family and later increasingly by peers. It is important to note that even if only one of the sexes is physically present in a family unit (e.g., a female parent with female children), the other sex will still be represented by subtle but powerful reciprocal attitudes and behaviors that are learned by family members in their interaction with other-sex peers, and by social images of that sex available in the culture (Money & Ehrhardt, 1972).

Proposition 3: Differentiation of sex roles within the family system is a significant factor influencing interaction patterns and communication sequences between family members.

Power hierarchies, boundaries, and patterns of meaning, or rules, that govern family behavior are all to some degree connected with sexual as well as with generational characteristics of family members. Both spousal and parent-child interaction patterns are, in part, reflections of attempts to live out socially scripted sex role behaviors and to influence significant others to do the same. Differentiation of self (i.e., development) is closely linked to sex role differentiation within the family system, since a major component of feedback on the social self of a family member consists of messages confirming or disconfirming gender identity and supporting or challenging sex-related role behaviors. In the final analysis, there is really no such thing as personality without sexuality. For example, by the time he reaches puberty, the boy socialized in the "macho" nonemotive image of masculinity will be seen by himself and others to have the qualities of reserve, stoicism, nonexpressiveness, and perhaps aggressiveness, that are associated with that sexual image.

Proposition 4: The family system organizes and expresses the embodiment of its members.

At the very minimum, a family unit must somehow find a way to ensure the physical survival of its members, which requires attending to their bodily needs and functions. This, in turn, confronts the family with the reality of its members' erotic (i.e., pleasure-seeking) capacities from birth onward (Gadpaille, 1975; Gagnon, 1977). All human experience is ultimately sensate experience, channeled through the body's sensory apparatus. The family system organizes the sensory experiences of its members, including the erotic components of those experiences, into meaningful patterns.

The importance of physical nurturance in the developmental process is widely acknowledged. The social recognition that comes with the exchange of affection between persons in close relationships is ego reinforcing to both of them. And the stimulation of pleasure centers, for example, through touch, appears to be an important factor in the bonding process (Harlow, 1974; Prescott, 1975).

Erotic behavior appears to develop out of hormonally mediated, periodically recurrent excitatory states that originate in an individual's central nervous system. These are gradually influenced and channeled by environmental forces—particularly within the family—until they occur at times, in places, and in response to stimuli that have become encoded within the brain of that individual as sexual (Money, 1980). Thus, family interaction gives meaning to biological events, influencing those events in certain ways not yet fully understood so that they become organized into the individual's developmental process as well as into the family's ongoing structure. The meaning of erotic expression to an individual—and the patterns of behavior that follow from it—are variations on the shared sexual meanings and behaviors of that individual's family system. From this it follows logically that behavior as organizationally complex as the choice of a romantic/erotic partner for pair bonding is a systemic phenomenon, reflecting multiple influences, rather than simply being the result of a single determining factor—for example, a mother with a particular personality, or the presence or absence of a father in the home.

Proposition 5: The nature and extent of sexual interaction among family members is largely a function of distance-regulating mechanisms in the family system and between the family system and its social environment.

As indicated above, both gender role behaviors and eroticism are fundamental and pervasive in family interaction patterns. However, since the family is a society's primary vehicle for organizing the sexual behavior of its citizens, much effort is put into codifying and regulating members' behavior within the family system. Regulatory maneuvers include both amplifications and limitations of expression. For example, family members may encourage the exaggeration of stereotyped sex role behaviors by an adolescent engaged in courtship while simultaneously discouraging touch or any erotically tinged interaction between that same adolescent and his or her parents.

In most cultures, genital expression within the family is reserved for the marital dyad. However, lesser degrees of erotic expression are acceptable in most family units: physical affection, grooming behaviors, partial or complete nudity, and verbal or written exchange of erotic information. There is no single normative prescription for erotic interaction patterns in the family. One can only infer an optimal balance between sexual detachment at one extreme and sexual enmeshment at the other—a balance of emotional and physical interaction that facilitates the differentiation of self by individual family members within the context of warm, supportive, nurturant relationships. Central to this process are appropriate physical boundaries (the integrity and privacy of the body) and psychological boundaries (respect for individual differences, emotional states, and freedom of decision making). In addition, it requires a recognition of the role-designated categorical boundaries of the family—member/nonmember, husband/wife, parent/child, brother/sister. There is evidence to suggest that families with overly rigid, insufficiently permeable environmental boundaries may experience a loosening of sexual boundaries within the family, creating a greater likelihood of psychological or physical incest between siblings or between parents and children (Larson, 1980).

Proposition 6: Sexual aspects of family experience are complexly related to other aspects of experience within the family system.

Sexual interaction patterns within the family powerfully affect members' behavior in other areas of family life and are, in turn, significantly affected by them. This results, in part, from the fact that family roles are strongly connected to the sexual and reproductive characteristics of members at various stages of the life cycle. It further derives from the powerful impact of sex role expectations on the personal identities (self-definitions) of family members.

This is illustrated in the role of sexual expression in the marital relationship. Research has consistently shown that sexual activity varies greatly in its contribution to the nature and quality of marital interaction (Hicks & Platt, 1971; Sager, 1976). On the one hand, sexual satisfaction and marital satisfaction are highly positively correlated. However, the nature of the relationship between them is uncertain in that both appear to interact with a complex, additive cluster of other factors, such as educational level of spouses, duration of marriage and number of children, etc. (Maison, 1981). As a result, it is virtually impossible to describe an optimal level or kind of sexual activity that would be generally applicable to marital dyads without regard to the particulars of their marital and family interaction patterns.

Children, too, manifest the effects of the complex relationships among sexuality, personal identity, and social roles within and outside the family. Rates of sexual maturation have been shown to have a strong impact on peer group social adjustment and resulting school behavior (Semmens & Krantz, 1970). And attitudes taken by parents toward their children's sex role characteristics have been found to profoundly influence a variety of aspects of development in both girls and boys (Kagan, 1976).

Proposition 7: The course of various stages in the family life cycle is strongly influenced by significant events in the individual psychosexual development of family members; conversely, patterns of psychosexual development of individual members are strongly influenced by qualities of corresponding stages in the family life cycle.

That sexual factors play a part in delineating stages of the family life cycle is quite apparent: romantic/erotic elements have a major role in initiating the family life cycle through marriage. Reproductive/erotic activities bring children into the system, which in turn frequently alters the sexual intimacy patterns of the marital dyad. Puberty and the accompanying changes in sex role expectations and potential for erotic expression mark the transition from the family with children to the family with adolescents. And the departure of the youngest adolescent from the immediate sphere of family influence—often to embark on his or her own romantic/erotic career—brings the family to the post-childbearing phase—a phase that frequently involves renegotiations of sexual intimacy patterns in the original marital partnership (Cleveland, 1976).

It is equally true, but perhaps less apparent, that factors in the family's life cycle stages have an impact on the course of members' psychosexual development. Money (1980) and other developmentalists have advanced the concept of a "critical period" in the elaboration of gender identity, erotic attachments, and even preferences for particular features of erotic interaction. This notion implies that the family system of which the developing individual is a member must be appropriately equipped to provide a supportive structure and complementary transaction patterns. The nature of the family's life cycle circumstances at a given stage of its development thus decidedly influences this sexual imprinting process.

Of course, everything may not proceed smoothly within the family system. The family does not always mark its transitions from stage to stage with open acknowledgment of sexual components and dynamics. The onset of first menstruation in the oldest girl may be celebrated as a symbol of reproductive maturity, while the sexual implications of her passage are only implied in the negative admonition to "be careful about being alone with a boy" (Maddock, 1973). Nevertheless, the shared meanings of sex within the family system often influence—sometimes dramatically—the nature and even the timing of family life-cycle transitions. For example, young married couples who invest a great deal of energy in the romantic/erotic/companionate aspect of their relationship may be influenced thereby to significantly postpone—perhaps even to eliminate altogether—their childbearing and childrearing activities. Or parents who psychosexually infantilize their postpubertal children may succeed, in one sense, in substantially prolonging the family's experience with the task of rearing adolescents. The reverse is also true. The physical development of the quickly maturing oldest child may precipitate a family's confrontation with adolescence long before other family members, especially parents, are prepared for it.

Proposition 8: Since the family is a highly "open" system, its sexual
meanings and accompanying behavior patterns are mutually
interactive with elements in its cultural-historical environment.

Like other aspects of family life, the dynamics of sex in a family system at a given point in time reflect a complex "family emotional field" spanning at least three generations (Bowen, 1978). Thus, a variety of cultural values and attitudes, some of them in conflict with each other, are likely to be held by various members of the family, or perhaps reflected in inconsistent attitudes of individual family members. Beliefs held by the older generations are likely to reflect homeostatic tendencies: "We didn't dress like that when we were your age." Change tendencies are more likely to be represented by the younger generations, particularly adolescents, whose peer orientation may lead them to bring diverse ideas into the family's shared sexual meaning system: "There is nothing wrong with it. All of my friends dress this way." Sexual attitudes represent an area of family values that are likely to shift often, as a result of developmental changes in the psychosexual needs of members and less predictable alterations in social mores.

Cultural ideas and attitudes may support and enhance the family's sexual structure and meaning system at a given point in time, as, for example, when religious or governmental institutions encourage procreation for newly married couples. But cultural values may also challenge the family's sexual meaning system, perhaps through educational institutions that provide programs encouraging young people to be tolerant of sexual life-style options their parents find morally offensive. And, occasionally, representatives of social institutions may even intervene directly into the family's conduct of its own sexual behavior, such as through legal prosecution of a family member for incestuous behavior that had been previously unchallenged within that family system. The permeable boundaries of the family system require that it continuously recalibrate its internal meanings and interactional processes in order to take into account the experiences of family members outside the system, as well as the circumstantial historical events of its cultural context.

CHARACTERISTICS OF THE SEXUALLY HEALTHY FAMILY

It is always easier to specify conditions of illness than to define health. Indeed, the concept of health is itself subject to changing social and cultural values and influenced by a wide variety of factors. Despite attempts to be encompassing, objective, and generic, every definition of health—including those of sexual health and family health—is inevitably composed of value-laden terms subject to many different interpretations. Nevertheless, it is important to attempt to draw some conclusions regarding normative principles for sexuality within the family system and in the context of the family life cycle.

Individual sexual health in the context of the life cycle may be seen as having four components:

1. The conviction that one's personal and social behaviors are congruent with one's gender identity, and a sense of comfort with a range of sex role behaviors.
2. The ability to carry on effective interpersonal relationships with members of both sexes, including the potential for love and long-term commitment.

3. The capacity to respond to erotic stimulation in such a way as to make sexual activity—including any activity that is not harmful or exploitative—a positive, pleasurable aspect of one's experience.
4. The maturity of judgment to make rewarding decisions about one's sexual behavior that do not conflict with one's overall value system and beliefs about life. (Maddock, 1975, p. 53)

These principles can be extended and integrated with the concepts outlined in the preceding propositions to yield a more elaborate series of normative principles defining the sexually healthy family:

Members of the sexually healthy family show mutual respect for both males and females and support congruence between each member's biologically given sex and her or his inner sense of gender identity.

Members of the sexually healthy family give recognition to sex role behaviors consistent with each member's inner sense of gender identity, while encouraging maximum flexibility in these behaviors consistent with effective social functioning inside and outside the family in a given cultural/historical context. (Here the key word is "effective." A family that encourages its members, particularly its children, to substantially deviate from cultural standards for sex-linked behaviors at a given point in history could risk compromising their physical, emotional, social, or economic well-being. The exact point at which this might occur is, of course, a matter of divergent opinion and a subject of current debate.)

Members of the sexually healthy family have a respectful appreciation for bodily functions and sensate experience, as well as for the unique physical attributes of each family member—all in an effort to promote a positive body/self-image in each member.

Members of the sexually healthy family have a respectful appreciation for the erotic response potential of each member at his or her particular stage of psychosexual development. The family system facilitates the expression of this capacity in responsible and appropriate ways rather than trying to restrain it unnecessarily.

The sexually healthy family encourages both practical and affectional touching and physical interaction among its members in stage-appropriate, nonexploitative ways.

The sexually healthy family has appropriate sexual boundaries that respect the physical and emotional privacy of each member while allowing for supportive, positive energy and information exchange when desired by family subsystems. These boundaries are clear and functional, though flexible and permeable, to allow for members' transactions and for appropriate adaptations to changing developmental needs.

The sexually healthy family communicates effectively about sex, using language that can accurately convey sexual information, reflect feelings and attitudes of members, and facilitate decision making and problem solving regarding sexual issues.

The marital partners in the sexually healthy family are secure in their personal sexual identities and exhibit an appropriate degree of flexibility in sexual role taking and role making. Coordination of decision making and problem solving extends comfortably and effectively across gender lines. Wife and husband convey to each other and to their children their respect and appreciation for their own and each other's sexuality, both gender role and erotic aspects.

The marital partners in the sexually healthy family participate in sexual and affectional interaction that is regarded as mutually rewarding. Their patterns of sexual exchange reflect freedom of choice and the capacity for negotiation, along with warmth, caring, and concern for each other's welfare. Their sexual relationship is based upon a sufficient degree of shared sexual meaning and interest to be considered satisfying to each. Included in their interaction is an agreed-upon system of responsibility for the reproductive potential and possible consequences of their sexual expression.

The sexually healthy family has a generational power structure in which appropriate guidance, protection, and support are supplied by the parents to permit the unfolding of childhood and adolescent sexuality in age-appropriate ways. The sexuality of younger members is respectfully nurtured rather than exploited to meet the needs of the older generation.

In the sexually healthy family, sexual values and attitudes are transmitted from one generation to the next primarily through positive interaction patterns in everyday life. However, the family also has at its disposal a body of accurate information about sexuality that can be shared between the generations and among members of the same generation, with appropriate consideration for the developmental stage of each family member.

Members of the sexually healthy family share an overall value system that permits effective and rewarding sexual decision making. This value system represents the uniqueness of the family as a unit while also sufficiently reflecting the family's community context.

The sexual value system of the sexually healthy family encourages autonomous decision making by family members consistent with respect for individuality but balanced by concern for the integrity of the family unit.

The social boundary of the sexually healthy family is semipermeable, permitting information exchange between the family and its environment so that it can remain meaningfully related to its cultural-historical context.

The sexually healthy family seeks the sexual differentiation of its members, allowing them to be as free as possible from "emotional fusion" with the "family ego mass" (Bowen, 1978). Transactions in the family are designed to foster the development of a solid sense of gender and self-identity, a comfortable range of sex role behaviors, erotic capacity, and freedom of choice regarding sexual life style. The sexually healthy family accepts the capacity of its members to appropriately represent its sexual integrity to the outside world.

The sexually healthy family system has the capacity for both first-order and second-order change. Because sexuality is a fundamental dimension of the family, because sexual events frequently accompany individual and family life cycle transitions, because sexual meanings and values fluctuate rapidly and significantly in the family's cultural-historical context—for all these reasons—it is a hallmark of sexual health that a family can master and adapt to new sexual circumstances inside and outside the family (first-order changes) and can also transform its sexual structure and meaning system to conform with more fundamental alteration in its sexual experience, for example, life cycle transitions (second-order changes). The inability of a family to change in relation to alterations in members' sexual experiences will eventually lead to symptom formation and family sexual "dis-ease."

FAMILY SEXUAL "DIS-EASE"

Issues are basic factors, or clusters of factors, in a family system that have demonstrable effect or outcome and importance for family members. Issues are always present in families, and they imply matters of choice for family members. *Problems* are issues that are not dealt with to the satisfaction of one or more family members at a given point in time. Problems are intermittently present in all families. *Symptoms* are undesirable, persistent or recurrent, internal experiences of an individual family member. They usually affect the individual's behavior, which in turn has an impact on other family members and on family issues, perhaps thereby contributing to family problems. *Family sexual dis-ease* refers to a cluster of sexual symptoms and/or problems within the family system.

Family-related sexual symptoms and problems will be addressed in detail in ensuing articles. Here we will only briefly summarize several theoretical principles underlying the experience of sexual problems and symptoms within the family. There are four clusters of factors producing sexual distress: intrapsychic, systemic, developmental, and situational.

Intrapsychic Factors

Intrapsychic factors are carried within adult family members as sources of disruption in the healthy expression of gender role behaviors or erotic interest. Developmental and systemic distresses in his or her family of origin create negative unconscious patterns within the adult individual, operating as an "imagistic memory bank" (Kantor & Lehr, 1975) that affects all transactions in the individual's current family. Examples are conflicts over gender identity, anxiety over homoerotic inclinations, or phobic reactions to genital function.

Systemic Factors

Systemic factors include dysfunction within the structure of the family system, that is, disruptions in family members' interaction patterns with regard to sexual issues:

Differential distance regulation by individual family members or by subsystems within the family, for example, conflicts over level of sexual interest or intensity of affectional interchange between spouses.

Role-definition ambiguities or conflicts between two or more family members, for example, parent-child disagreements over differential rule setting for male and female adolescents.

Sexual boundary diffusion (enmeshment) between family members, for example, adoption of the maternal role by an adolescent girl, whose father then generalizes the role behavior to include incestuous sexual contact.

Sexual boundary rigidity (detachment) between family members, leading to stimulus and touch deprivation, social isolation, body image anxiety, etc.

Dysfunctional communication patterns with respect to sexual issues, for example, lack of a cross-generational language system to permit parent-child interchanges regarding sexual decision making.

Disruption of established power hierarchies within the family or within subsystems, for example, a challenge to a husband's decision-making authority by his wife resulting in inhibited sexual desire or dysfunction.

Lack of sufficient flexibility to adapt to new or unique sex-related phenomena or events introduced into the system, for example, the offering of a school sex education program precipitating intrafamily conflict.

Lack of capacity to transform family structure in response to predictable or unpredictable major life crises, for example, when illness or injury permanently affecting the sexual function, body image, and role behavior of a family member is ignored by other family members.

Developmental Factors

Developmentally dysfunctional factors in the family result from the inability of the system to cope effectively with various kinds of change:

Transitions from one developmental stage to another may require structural transformations in the family's sexual system. When this fails to occur, the family is left with familiar, but ineffective, ways to interact with respect to sexual issues, for example, parents who "ground" an adolescent girl in a futile effort to prevent contact with a boyfriend of whom they do not approve.

Dislocations in the life cycle of an individual family member may require modification in the structure of sex-related transactions in the family and may affect the course of development of one or more other family members; for example, the pregnancy of an unmarried teen-age girl may tax the family's resources for emotional support, may trigger reactionary restrictions on the social behavior of younger siblings, or may even precipitate a family life cycle transition if the parents are left without children at home following a premature "launching" of their daughter into marriage.

Dislocations in the family life cycle challenge the system to restructure itself as well as altering the normal course of development of one or more family members; for example, parents of nearly grown children who were enjoying the reestablishment of a more active sexual relationship may be required to recycle through the parenting stages if an unexpected mid-life pregnancy occurs.

Situational Factors

Situational factors underlying sexual distress include those that occur largely outside the family system but that may have some indirect effect on the system via their effects on one or more members; and those that occur inside the family as a single, random behavioral event rather than as a transactional pattern. An example of the former is the temporary upset in response to the chance exposure of a child on the way home from school to an exhibitionistic stranger. The latter is illustrated by the single occasion of erectile failure experienced by a fatigued husband with his wife following a late night party. Even something as circumstantial as the placement of the marital bed against a thin wall of an adjoining apartment can precipitate sexual distress that comes to the attention of the clinician. However, it is important to remember that a situational factor can become a systemic or developmental variable if it should acquire sufficient meaning to one or more family members or if it is repeated over time and becomes patterned.

SEX IN THE FAMILY LIFE CYCLE

Numerous family life cycle frameworks have been advanced (Duvall, 1962; Haley, 1973; Hill, 1970; Rodgers, 1962), each characterized by varying numbers of stages tied to entrances and exits of family members and to stages in their individual life cycles—many of which, as noted above, reflect an aspect of sexuality. All of these developmental schemas imply the periodic restructuring of the family system in line with the changing needs and circumstances of its members, individually and collectively. Carter and McGoldrick (1980) have presented a six-stage framework (Table 1-1) that can serve as a basis for observations on the sexual dynamics of the family life cycle.

1. The Unattached Young Adult: Courtship

Courtship is a process of exploring options for commitment, followed by the building of intimacy patterns through social and sexual experimentation.

Table 1-1 The Stages of the Family Life Cycle

Family Life Cycle Stage	Emotional Process of Transition: Key Principles	Second Order Changes in Family Status Required to Proceed Developmentally
1. Between Families: The Unattached Young Adult	Accepting parent offspring separation	a. Differentiation of self in relation to family of origin b. Development of intimate peer relationships c. Establishment of self in work
2. The Joining of Families Through Marriage: The Newly Married Couple	Commitment to new system	a. Formation of marital system b. Realignment of relationships with extended families and friends to include spouse
3. The Family With Young Children	Accepting new members into the system	a. Adjusting marital system to make space for child(ren) b. Taking on parenting roles c. Realignment of relationships with extended family to include parenting and grandparenting roles
4. The Family With Adolescents	Increasing flexibility of family boundaries to include children's independence	a. Shifting of parent child relationships to permit adolescent to move in and out of system b. Refocus on mid-life marital and career issues c. Beginning shift toward concerns for older generation
5. Launching Children and Moving On	Accepting a multitude of exits from and entries into the family system	a. Renegotiation of marital system as a dyad b. Development of adult to adult relationships between grown children and their parents c. Realignment of relationships to include in-laws and grandchildren d. Dealing with disabilities and death of parents (grandparents)
6. The Family in Later Life	Accepting the shifting of generational roles	a. Maintaining own and/or couple functioning and interests in face of physiological decline; exploration of new familial and social role options b. Support for a more central role for middle generation c. Making room in the system for the wisdom and experience of

Table 1-1 Continued

Family Life Cycle Stage	Emotional Process of Transition: Key Principles	Second Order Changes in Family Status Required to Proceed Developmentally
		the elderly; supporting the older generation without overfunctioning for them
		d. Dealing with loss of spouse, siblings and other peers and preparation for own death. Life review and integration

Source: "The Family Life Cycle and Family Therapy: An Overview" by Elizabeth A. Carter and Monica McGoldrick, in Carter and McGoldrick, *The Family Life Cycle: A Framework for Family Therapy.* New York: Gardner Press, 1980. Reprinted with permission.

Interaction patterns are begun, dropped, or revised, and gradually developed into stable configurations. Individual boundaries are examined and tested to see if they will facilitate exchange of information and emotional energy without either rigidifying or collapsing.

Erik Erikson (1959) has noted that genuine emotional intimacy is not possible between partners until ego identity has formed to a sufficient degree to permit exchange without loss, giving without giving up, and sharing of identity without identity diffusion. One major component of identity is gender identity and the role behaviors that are linked to it. Therefore, one of the major components of the intimacy building process in courtship is the mutual confirmation of role identities, that is, of respective versions of maleness and femaleness. Gender role complementarity is far more crucial in mate selection than erotic compatibility. However, the erotic aspect has some early importance as well. It relates to the emotional energy—the "spark" of passion—that motivates the partners toward closeness and cooperation. It is one of the important factors that reassures them that the ensuing effort of maintaining a commitment is worthwhile. In addition, the nature, degree, and results of whatever premarital erotic experimentation is chosen by the partners already reflect their capacity for negotiation as well as for mutuality without loss of ego boundaries (Maddock, 1973).

Couples who bring sex role compatibility problems to clinicians before marriage do well to resolve them before proceeding, for left unsettled they will severely affect the "balance of power" underlying the entire relationship. The clinician encountering unmarried partners with disputes or dysfunctions in the erotic realm is very likely observing not a problem of mechanics, but a difficulty with either autonomy or commitment. Here the body and/or the libido are commentators on the readiness of the partners for genuine intimacy. Finally, some couples may experience problems by being sexually precocious, placing the task of sexual adjustment in a committed relationship ahead of the decision to commit.

2. The Newly Married Couple

The first stage of marriage is both continuous and discontinuous with the courtship process. Interaction patterns are still being developed and revised, but with some important differences. The system's boundary has now become more closed; more is expected to be accomplished within the confines of the marital system—yet the marriage has brought together two families, each with its own structures and roles, and the stage is set for conflict. Purposes have also changed now that the marriage has begun. Coordination of immediate objectives as well as long-range goals becomes more necessary. The marital system's capacity for reciprocity—still somewhat new and unfamiliar—will now be tested.

Newly married couples are especially susceptible to pressure from sex role standards, both those in the society at large and the internalized versions learned in their respective families of origin. Hearing the terms "husband" and "wife" from each other as well as their families and friends, they are likely to feel obligated to behave in ways that have been conveyed to them by these images. Yet they are also under pressure to have loosened themselves somewhat from their same-sex peer support systems (just as from their families) in order to be more fully available physically and emotionally to each other. Trouble can occur if either or both violate this assumption, for example, by spending too much time out with "the girls" or "the boys." All in all, they have embarked on a challenging venture. Everything he has learned and become as a male and everything she has learned and become as a female are expected to blend together in a complementary and coordinated fashion to become a smoothly operating, efficient, and personally satisfying mechanism known as a "marriage."

The marital bed is expected to reflect the dynamics of the rest of the marital system. Often it does, to the dismay of one or both partners. Erotically, they are challenged to adjust not so much to each other's sexual behavior as to each other's—and their own—sexual expectations. Complex messages and memories from families and early life experiences lurk in the background or come unexpectedly to the fore. Variations and discrepancies in their sexual desires begin to surface and require negotiated adjustments into a mutually satisfying pattern. Sharing of sexual meanings becomes more important over time than the logistics of sexual activity. The relative importance of sex to each of the partners has a great deal to do with how this area is structured into the overall marital system—and to what degree sex comes to be a major arena for, on the positive side, meeting of intimacy needs or, on the negative side, struggling for power.

Crucial to sexual success in the early years of marriage are sufficient differentiation from one's family of origin to permit physical and emotional vulnerability, self-worth reflected in body comfort, the capacity for reality testing and adjustment of expectations, assertiveness and the ability to negotiate personal wants and desires, and a suitable language system to conduct such negotiations. Couples lacking one or more of these characteristics are likely to present themselves in therapy or, alternatively, to develop problems that generalize to other relationship areas and could lead to marital dissolution.

3. The Family with Young Children

To some degree, parenthood has come to be viewed as a choice, an option that couples are exercising less often currently than in the past, and, in some cases, not at all (Blake, 1979). The separation of procreation from erotic activity coincides with an increased emphasis in marriage on personal fulfillment and companionship that replaces the more traditional stress on economic and childrearing functions (Lederer & Jackson, 1968). This, in turn, has heightened the awareness of the implications of "making space" for children in a marriage and the resultant increase in complexity in family system dynamics.

However, few couples embarking on parenthood anticipate the sex-related implications of their choice. That household roles and rules will be affected by the entry of children is to some degree expected; that individual sexual attitudes and shared sexual values will be substantially altered is not. Of the myriad and complicated ways in which this occurs, only several of the more prominent will be briefly mentioned here.

Perhaps the most noticeable shift in the life routine of parents with young children is their sacrifice of personal time and privacy. Patterns of erotic and affectional interchange are among the most likely to be altered and sometimes severely disrupted if there is not sufficient security and flexibility to permit a satisfactory reconciliation of personal needs and parental responsibilities.

Gender identity is so taken for granted (though becoming less so) that many parents do not notice how patterns of family interaction are strongly influenced by gender-related characteristics and behavior of members. Interaction with children, or with a spouse regarding childrearing issues, may force a parent to confront deeply internalized stereotypes and expectations of his or her own or the opposite sex. This is especially true when such a confrontation challenges the adult's unconscious wish to replicate herself or himself in a child. Such hidden agendas tend to be worked out largely along sex-related lines within the family, producing a variety of coalitions, triangles, and conflict patterns that revolve around the genders of the participants and their associated behaviors.

From birth onward, children create interaction patterns in the family that are physical, sensual, and even erotic, but that are bounded by restrictions against genital expression. The family with small children is already challenged to strike a balance in fostering erotic potential through positive body experiences while protecting its smaller members from excessive vulnerability and exploitation, both inside and outside the family circle. Families failing to find this balance may present the clinician with a range of sex-related problems, from incest to marital dysfunction to bizarre sexual symptomatology in one or more children.

The family with children is challenged to have a version of sexuality that can be shared among members, in both verbal and nonverbal ways. This includes overall values about sex in human life, views on the meaning and significance of gender, interpretations of bodily functions and sensate experiences, attitudes toward the wide variety of sexual phenomena to be encountered outside the family, and information on what to expect as physical, social, and emotional maturation proceeds. "Where did I come from?" is ultimately an existential question that the child will ask repeatedly in different forms and for which he or she will devise an answer even if parents avoid explicit response. Significant deficits in childhood sexual socialization may bring an adult into therapy for some family-of-origin work.

4. The Family with Adolescents

As Erikson (1968) and others have pointed out, adolescent identity formation is a reciprocal process of mutual recognition by the young person and his or her society. Thus, adolescence might best be defined as a developmental experience directed toward taking one's place as a recognized, and recognizable, individual in a particular social and historical setting.

The family remains a crucial mechanism in the recognition process, although the influence of peers increases dramatically. A state of tension is created, both within the adolescent and within the family, as a result of the overlapping boundaries of family system and peer system in the life of the adolescent. This is marked by great instability, with constantly changing patterns of influence and action, by shifting coalitions, and by psychological forces pushing alternately toward dependence and independence. Families with adolescents have their boundaries and structures challenged, and members often feel intruded upon by the adolescent and his or her peers. Particularly in modern Western cultures, adolescence is a highly complex social phenomenon, extending in both directions well beyond the teen-age years. As a result, the family with adolescents is placed into a protracted state of stress, challenged to transform itself in a particularly significant way to meet changing conditions (Ackerman, 1980).

Among the imperatives the adolescent faces is that of asserting sexual identity in a manner compatible with gender role characteristics and erotic inclinations. While developmentally continuous with the sexual experience of the individual since birth, sexual expression in adolescence is specifically characterized by the necessity of integrating mature genitality—and thus reproductive possibilities—into an as yet incomplete personality structure. The dynamics of this internal conflict make sex a primary focus of the adolescent agony of self-consciousness (Maddock, 1973). Biological factors are only the broad limits of the presence and patterning of sexuality in adolescence. More powerful are the psychosocial meanings attached to various behaviors by the individual. Here is where the adequacy of previous preparation by the family is demonstrated. Entering adolescence grossly lacking in information, emotional orientation, and supportive socialization regarding appropriate gender role behaviors and erotic possibilities, the individual is at risk for rejection or exploitation by peers. By contrast, if the individual is overly enmeshed in the eroticism of the family or has been channeled into a rigidly defined gender role identity, she or he is in danger of being unable to endure the give-and-take of mutual recognition required for identity formation in the larger social context. Again the result is social rejection or self-imposed isolation. Such an individual may never truly leave home, either psychologically or, less often but more noticeably, geographically as well.

Regarding sexuality, the family with adolescents is challenged to strike a balance between helpless permissiveness and reactionary rigidity. Adolescent children will *not* behave sociosexually exactly as did their parents or grandparents; their generational context is too different to allow that. However, the overall sexual attitudes and values between the generations in a given family remain remarkably consistent (Reiss, 1971). The developmental context is itself responsible for some of the discrepancies of attitudes and behavior within the family, that is, the tasks of adolescence are by definition exploratory and experimental, requiring the adolescent to search out options before committing and settling down. By contrast, the tasks of parenting are those of responsibility, continuity, and stability. Small wonder, then, that adolescents tend to express the most liberal sexual attitudes of their lifetimes, while parents of adolescents are likely to be at their most conservative (Reiss, 1971).

Parents with adolescents have a particularly good opportunity to explicitly share something of their sexuality with their children. Of course, this has been done all along in a variety of implicit, mostly nonverbal ways. Now, however, if the stage has been well set, there will be opportunities to talk. Conversations about sexuality conducted sensitively, supportively, and without undue intrusiveness can help maintain family cohesiveness even as a developmentally necessary loosening of parent-child dependency is taking place. Adolescents are more secure in their own struggle for autonomy when they know where their parents stand on important sex-related issues, even if they do not choose precisely the same attitudes for themselves. Parents who are most secure in their own sexual identities will be best equipped to foster the independent sexual identities of their children. They will not need to keep them "all in the family," but will appreciate sharing with the larger community the individuals they have produced and nurtured toward selfhood.

Therapists see families with adolescents primarily with respect to two broad categories of difficulties: intergenerational conflicts, and problems associated with the adolescents preparing to leave home (Haley, 1980). Commonly, these problems reflect sexual issues. Sometimes they are explicit and suggest sex as a fruitful avenue of clinical focus; often, they are implicit, hidden among accounts of rebellious behavior, school performance problems, and emotional disorders. It is important to address them in any form.

5. Launching Children and Moving On

To the naive observer, the family that has launched its adolescent children may have the appearance of a system returning to a previous state. Of course, this is not the case. Adults who have reared children will never again have their preparental identities; nor will they interact as in earlier years, except with the most superficial similarity. After the last child has left home, the marital dyad is not *re*-formed, but once again *trans*-formed.

As the children leave home, whatever gender-linked differentiation of tasks that occurred in connection with childrearing is reexamined and altered to suit the new realities of time, space, and privacy. Emotional patterns of interchange are more difficult to transform. Supportive coalitions and subsystems that involved the children—some formed along same-gender lines and others across gender—begin to shift. Frequently, these emotional coalitions persist and influence behavior patterns between the parents and their married children now living in other households. The gender-related aspects of these coalitions may be very obvious, as, for example, when a married woman returns home to spend an evening or weekend talking with her mother, while her husband and his father-in-law are left to evolve a program of compatible activity (such as watching football on television or playing golf). Other gender-associated characteristics are powerful but subtle and may be revealed only under certain circumstances, such as in marital therapy when one spouse admits to judging negatively the actions of the other, comparing the spouse's behavior with the behavior of an admired parent of the other sex.

Facilitating the task for grown children leaving home (both physically and psychologically) requires that parents be satisfied enough with the job they have done in childrearing that they are not tempted to continue treating their grown offspring as children in a remedial effort. Naturally, certain events can cause this confidence to be shaken. For example, the "coming out" process of gay adult children is widely recognized to trigger parental anxiety, no matter how liberal these same parents may be in their overall sexual attitudes (Bell & Weinberg, 1978).

Adults whose children have left home have the chance to establish a pattern of more intense romantic and erotic involvement. Some welcome this as an opportunity for increased companionship, even "courtship." Others retain behavior patterns—including sexual activities—that were established during the childrearing years because they reflect a comfortable combination of autonomy and intimacy for the particular individuals involved. Still others begin a pattern of heightened conflict based, in part, upon the knowledge that opportunities for closer interaction are present but not desired by one or both partners. Without the buffering effect of interpersonal triangles involving the children, unresolved disputes and deep-seated resentments may begin to surface. These may involve sex: perhaps a move toward power or autonomy by a spouse who has felt oppressed by her or his role in the family system, or perhaps the expression of long-contained anger about the lack of affectional and erotic intimacy that may have characterized the marriage during the childrearing years. If emotional or erotic affairs have been conducted outside the marriage while the children were in the home, their exit may be a signal for the destabilization of that triangle, which could precipitate conflict and possible divorce.

All in all, partners in the post-childrearing years have the opportunity to explore the possibilities of a mature, committed intimate relationship as at no other time in their developmental sequence. This will be hampered, perhaps even prevented, if maladaptive family transactions cause one or both parents to hold on to children (whether in or out of the home) for emotional support. Conversely, one or more of the children may be prevented from departing because of a subliminal sense that he or she would be abandoning parents to conflict or unhappiness. Therapists have often seen adolescents or young adults remaining with their parents to aid one parent in preventing discovery of an extramarital affair or to protect the other parent from the pain that such discovery would bring.

6. The Family in Later Life

Attention is finally being given to the sexual aspects of later life and of the aging process (Butler & Lewis, 1977; Starr & Weiner, 1981).There has been a tendency for society to place little emphasis on the gender-linked role behaviors of individuals past the childrearing years. The results of this are both positive and negative. On the one hand, it has liberated some older individuals from the restrictions of sex role stereotypes, permitting, for example, older women to work outside the home free from the image of damaging relationships in the family or in the marketplace. On the other hand, this desexualization has been shown to create lowered self-esteem in many older people by making them seem less attractive and less effective as persons (Starr & Weiner, 1981).

Particularly powerful has been the tendency to deny the erotic potential of the later years. Research has now demonstrated that it is physical health and overall activity level, rather than chronological age, that determine the capacity of the individual for sexual function (Woods, 1979). Likewise, the availability of a regularly interested, and interesting, sexual partner appears to be the major determinant of the role that sexual activity will play in the relationship of older spouses (Masters & Johnson, 1966). Of course, the aging process and accompanying physical or health difficulties often alter the nature of sexual activity. The older couple is challenged to creatively adapt to changing circumstances in their sexual relationship; unfortunately, many have neither the inclination to do so nor the benefit of previous comfort and flexibility regarding sex to help them. Maintenance of erotic activity appears to provide a certain spark of vitality and motivation—even pride—for many older couples, a pride that is sometimes shared and at other times disparaged by their grown children.

Faced with threats of illness and death, body integrity can become a matter of considerable importance to older individuals. Compliments on appearance, affectionate touch, and erotic expression are thus particularly powerful channels of communication between partners. Important also are the physical proximity and affectionate gestures of children and grandchildren. Overall, then, physical modes of interaction can take on renewed importance in the family system in later life, up to and including the dying process itself.

Many older adults become somewhat more tolerant during the last few years of their lives, including their attitudes about sexual matters. They have had enough experience to have gained considerable wisdom. In their own way, many older individuals and couples are open to change, perhaps only because it brings with it possibilities for renewal that may in some way prolong life. Thus, they can be valuable as the third generation in the family system, passing on to their children (who are now quite likely to have teen-age or young adult children of their own) some of the benefits of their experience. They are also likely to be repositories of information regarding family rules and rituals.

Oldest family members are valuable resources for family therapy, including work on sex-related problems. At that stage in life, they may be willing to bring forth long-held secrets of the extended family, including such things as failed courtships, premarital pregnancies, extramarital affairs, and even unusual sexual practices suspected or confirmed. But more important, aging adults are links to the family's history and to the more distant aspects of its cultural context; they can, therefore, provide a constant source of influence on the younger generations regarding their family's own unique version of what it means to be a female or a male in ways that have helped the family survive with integrity.

CONCLUSION

A great deal of technical information about sex is readily available to readers in a variety of recent sources (e.g., Francoeur, 1982; Money & Musaph, 1977; Sadock, Kaplan, & Freedman, 1976). Instead of focusing on this information or on specific sexual problems in family life—which will be dealt with in the subsequent articles—this article has presented a way of thinking about human sexuality in relation to the family system and the family life cycle. Not all of the principles outlined are scientifically well validated. However, they are derived directly or indirectly from widely recognized work on human behavior from a variety of perspectives and have been verified to a considerable degree in clinical work with families. Because they are useful guidelines for finding meaningful patterns of inter-action in families, they provide a framework for considering the information on sexual problems in family therapy presented in the remainder of this book. In addition, it is hoped that they may contribute to furthering the acceptance of sexuality as an integral component of the family system throughout its life cycle, and, in turn, to advances in family theory construc-tion and to improvement in the effectiveness of family therapy.

REFERENCES

Ackerman, N.J. The family with adolescents. In E.A. Carter & M. McGoldrick (Eds.), *The family life cycle: A framework for family therapy*. New York: Gardner, 1980.

Andolfi, M. *Family therapy: An interactional approach*. New York: Plenum, 1979.

Annon, J. *The behavioral treatment of sexual problems* (Vols. I & II). Honolulu: Enabling Systems, 1975.

Bell, A.P., & Weinberg, M.S. *Homosexualities*. New York: Simon & Schuster, 1978.

Blake, J. Is zero preferred? American attitudes toward childlessness in the 1970s. *Journal of Marriage and Family*, 1979, *41*(2), 245-257.

Bowen, M. *Family therapy in clinical practice*. New York: Jason Aronson, 1978.

Buckley, W. (Ed.). *Modern systems research for the behavioral scientist*. Chicago: Aldine, 1968.

Butler, R.N., & Lewis, M.J. *Love and sex after sixty*. New York: Harper & Row, 1977.

Carter, E.A., & McGoldrick, M. (Eds.). *The family life cycle: A framework for family therapy*. New York: Gardner, 1980.

Cleveland, M. Sex and marriage at forty and beyond. *Family Coordinator*, 1976, *25*(2), 233-240.

Duvall, E.M. *Family development*. Philadelphia: Lippincott, 1962.

Edel, A. *Ethical judgment: The use of science in ethics*. Glencoe, Ill.: Free Press, 1955.

Erikson, E.H. *Childhood and society*. New York: Norton, 1950.

Erikson, E.H. Identity and the life cycle. *Psychological Issues*, I (1). New York: International Universities Press, 1959.

Erikson, E.H. *Identity: Youth and crisis*. New York: Norton, 1968.

Francoeur, R.T. *Becoming a sexual person*. New York: Wiley, 1982.

Gadpaille, W. *The cycles of sex*. New York: Charles Scribner's Sons, 1975.

Gagnon, J. *Human sexualities*. Glenview, Ill.: Scott, Foresman, 1977.

Gould, R.L. *Transformations: Growth and change in adult life*. New York: Simon & Schuster, 1978.

Haley, J. *Uncommon therapy: The psychiatric techniques of Milton H. Erickson, M.D*. New York: Norton, 1973.

Haley, J. *Leaving home: The therapy of disturbed young people*. New York: McGraw-Hill, 1980.

Harlow, H.F. *Learning to love*. New York: Jason Aronson, 1974.

Henley, N. *Body politics: Power, sex and nonverbal communication*. New York: Prentice-Hall, 1977.

Hicks, M., & Platt, M. Marital happiness and stability: A review of the research in the sixties. In C. Broderick (Ed.), *A decade of family research and action*. Minneapolis: National Council on Family Relations, 1971, 49-86.

Hill, R. *Family development in three generations*. Cambridge, Mass.: Schenkman, 1970.

Hoffman, L. *Foundations of family therapy*. New York: Basic Books, 1981.

Kagan, J. Psychology of sex differences. In F. Beach (Ed.), *Human sexuality in four perspectives*. Baltimore: Johns Hopkins University Press, 1976.

Kantor, D., & Lehr, W. *Inside the family*. San Francisco: Jossey-Bass, 1975.

Kaplan, H.S. *The new sex therapy*. New York: Brunner/Mazel, 1974.

Larson, N.R. An analysis of the effectiveness of a state-sponsored program designed to teach intervention skills in the treatment of family sexual abuse (Doctoral dissertation, University of Minnesota, 1980). Ann Arbor: Dissertation Abstracts.

Lederer, W.J., & Jackson, D.D. *The mirages of marriage*. New York: Norton, 1968.

Levinson, D. *The seasons of a man's life*. New York: Knopf, 1978.

LoPiccolo, J., and LoPiccolo, L. (Eds.). *Handbook of sex therapy*. New York: Plenum, 1978.

Maddock, J.W. Sex in adolescence: Its meaning and its future. *Adolescence*, 1973, *8*(31), 325-342.

Maddock, J.W. Sexual health and health care. *Postgraduate Medicine*, 1975, *58*, 52-58.

Maison, S. Factors affecting the relationship between sexual and marital satisfaction (Doctoral dissertation, University of Minnesota, 1981). Ann Arbor: Dissertation Abstracts.

Masters W., & Johnson, V. *Human sexual response*. Boston: Little, Brown, 1966.

Masters, W., & Johnson, V. *Human sexual inadequacy*. Boston: Little, Brown, 1970.

Minuchin, S., Rosman, B., & Baker, L. *Psychosomatic families*. Cambridge, Mass.: Harvard University Press, 1978.

Money, J. *Love and love sickness*. Baltimore: Johns Hopkins University Press, 1980.

Money, J., & Ehrhardt, A. *Man & woman/boy & girl*. Baltimore: Johns Hopkins University Press, 1972.

Money, J., & Musaph, H. (Eds.). *Handbook of sexology*. New York: Excerpta Medica, 1977.

Nelson, J.B. *Embodiment: An approach to sexuality and Christian theology*. Minneapolis: Augsburg, 1978.

Neugarten, B.L. Adult personality: Toward a psychology of the life cycle. In W.E. Vinacke (Ed.), *Readings in general psychology*. New York: American Book Company, 1968.

Olson, D.H., Russell, C.S., & Sprenkle, D.H. Circumplex model of marital and family systems. I: Cohesion and adaptability dimensions, family types and clinical applications. *Family Process*, 1979, *18*, 3-28.

Petras, J.W. *Sexuality in society* (2nd ed.). Boston: Allyn & Bacon, 1980.

Prescott, J.W. Body pleasure and the origins of violence. *The Futurist*, April 1975, 64-74.

Reiss, I.L. Premarital sex codes: The old and the new. In D.L. Grummon & A.M. Barclay (Eds.), *Sexuality: Search for perspective*. New York: Van Nostrand, 1971.

Rodgers, R. *Improvements in the construction and analysis of family life cycle categories.* Kalamazoo: Western Michigan University Press, 1962.

Sadock, B., Kaplan, H., & Freedman, A. (Eds.). *The sexual experience*. Baltimore: Williams & Wilkins, 1976.

Sager, C. Sex as a reflection of the total relationship. *Journal of Sex and Marital Therapy*, 1976, *2*(1), 3-5.

Semmens, J.P. & Krantz, K.E. *The adolescent experience*. New York: Macmillan, 1970.

Starr, B.D., & Weiner, M.B. *The Starr-Weiner report on sex and sexuality in the mature years.* New York: Stein & Day, 1981.

Terkelson, K.G. Toward a theory of the family life cycle. In E.A. Carter & M. McGoldrick (Eds.), *The family life cycle: A framework for family therapy*. New York: Gardner, 1980.

Tillich, P. *Systematic theology* (Vol.3). Chicago: University of Chicago Press, 1963.

Watzlawick, P., Weakland, J., & Fisch, R. *Change: Principles of problem formation and problem resolution*. New York: Norton, 1974.

Woods, N.F. *Human sexuality in health and illness* (2nd ed.). St. Louis: C.V. Mosby, 1979.

2. The Sexual Self and Fertility

Diane B. Brashear, PhD
Brashear Center, Inc.
Indiana University School of Social Work
Indianapolis, Indiana

John L. Ebling, MSW
Metro Health Plan
Brashear Center, Inc.
Indianapolis, Indiana

> And God blessed them, and God said unto them, be fruitful, and
> multiply, and replenish the earth and subdue it . . . (Genesis
> 1:27-28)

THE DUALISTIC NATURE OF HUMAN SEXUALITY HAS HAD A GENESIS of its own. There has long been a moral imperative associated with the procreative aspect of sexuality. It was sanctioned by the legal and moral institutions of Western culture for centuries and embodied in the rites associated with marriage and the roles ascribed to the traditional family. A similar degree of positive sanction has not been associated with the pleasure aspect of sexuality. Indeed, the physiological and psychological dynamics of male and female sexual pleasure have only recently emerged as a focus of professional and scientific inquiry.

Moral issues associated with sexual pleasure are the focus of considerable debate as social institutions struggle to define the limits of acceptable sexual behavior. In recent years the issue has been addressed by an attempt to establish, or reestablish, parameters of behavior associated with fertility—contraceptive use and availability, abortion, artificial insemination, conception in vitro, surrogate pregnancy. The victors of these debates will have succeeded in establishing important social and legal parameters of procreative and pleasurable sexual behavior for the majority of society for years to come.

Periods in social history during which there exists an essential unanimity regarding moral directives are characterized by relative social stability and compliance. However, inevitably social processes emerge and exert destabilizing influences that lead to social change. One such change agent is technology. With the advent of the age of technology in the twentieth century, the traditional and persistent division of labor in Western culture was both challenged and transformed. Cultural subscription to biological determinism had relegated child-raising functions to the woman and provider status to the man, but technology progressively freed both men and women from necessary tasks that had previously required the expenditure of considerable time and energy. Aside from economic and cultural barriers related to sex, race, ethnicity, and religious preference, individuals could now express themselves and seek fulfillment through endeavors beyond those dictated by prescribed roles.

With the discovery of practical, effective, and relatively safe methods of birth control, individuals were afforded a larger measure of personal control over their own fertility. With the acquisition of the means by which pregnancy could be avoided, the number and frequency of pregnancies could be regulated by the individual. One no longer had to abstain from sexual intercourse for fear of unwanted pregnancy. Men and women became, in effect, free to pursue sexual pleasure, constrained only by their own sense of propriety.

The significance of men and women acquiring convenient means by which fertility could be regulated has profound historical importance. Indeed, Montague (1969) has compared the social significance of the pill to that of the discovery of fire and tools by primitive groups, the development of urbanism, the life-saving discoveries of scientific medicine, and the harnessing of nuclear energy. Technology provided the means to facilitate an individual's intended goal with respect to procreativity. Like other options, childbearing became dependent upon the degree of one's personal freedom, awareness, knowledge, and sense of responsibility, all within the parameters of physiological reproductive capacity, and influenced by social and relational contextual factors.

The birth control methods, leisure time, and relative freedom of mobility, combined with the social effects of advances of women and minorities in recent decades, have challenged the traditional roles within society to the extent that relative unanimity with respect to pleasurable and procreative sexual conduct seems no longer apparent. It is increasingly evident that for any given life style there exist counterstyles, with any and all professing some semblance of moral justification and the right to act in accordance with their convictions. The resultant cacophony can be quite unsettling for those individuals, couples, and families struggling with the myriad issues surrounding the decision to have children.

The client, couple, or family who presents with a fertility problem is likely to demonstrate evidence of varying degrees of anxiety, ambivalence, misinformation, or, in some cases, depression. Some may be in active crisis. Couples and families may reveal disparate agendas with respect to fertility or one or both partners might lack the communication skills needed to convey their individual thoughts and feelings in order to achieve a satisfactory mutual understanding. Optimal intervention requires that the professional be essentially familiar with both male and female reproductive physiology and contraceptive methods, as well as with the plethora of possible issues surrounding fertility during each of the phases of the life cycle. While an extensive discussion of sexual physiology is beyond the scope of this article, some theoretical and therapeutic approaches will be provided with respect to the following topics: adolescent sexuality and fertility, managing fertility in the committed or marital relationship, coping with unwanted pregnancy, issues concerning infertility, and issues concerning the decision to have no children.

ADOLESCENT SEXUALITY AND FERTILITY

And so women get ready for procreation quite early; in fact one of the important problems of adolescence is how to avoid the accident of procreation. (Harry Stack Sullivan, 1953, p. 66)

The Alan Guttmacher Institute (1981) estimates that some five million young women and seven million young men in our society between the ages of 13 and 19 are sexually active today. Adolescents begin sexual activity, on the average, around the age of 16. The relationship between contraceptive use and adolescent pregnancy is staggering: roughly 62% of those who never use a method of birth control experience premarital pregnancy, while only 30% of those who employ methods inconsistently and 7% of those who consistently employ a medically prescribed method—diaphragm, the pill, or IUD —become pregnant (Zelnik & Kanter, 1979). It is estimated that more than 1 in 10 teen-agers become pregnant each year, and if current trends are not abated, 4 in 10 adolescent females who are now 14 will become pregnant at least once while still in their teens (Alan Guttmacher Institute, 1981).

In 1976, it was determined that nearly two-thirds of unwed adolescent women who were sexually active either did not employ a contraceptive method or used a method inconsistently. Forty-one percent believed they could not get pregnant, usually because they assumed that intercourse occurred during an infertile phase of their menstrual cycle. The major reason given for not using contraception by those who realized they could get pregnant was that they had not expected to have intercourse. Approximately 8% wanted to use a method but said they were not knowledgeable about contraception, or where to obtain appropriate information, or believed they could not "under the circumstances" use birth control (Alan Guttmacher Institute, 1981).

Clearly, these facts are indicative of an extensive lack of knowledge regarding fertility and contraceptive use on the part of today's adolescents. It is also evidence of their limited personal awareness with respect to sexuality. Given these conclusions and the present epidemic of adolescent pregnancy, an understanding of adolescent sexuality by the practicing therapist is crucial.

Eros, Lust, and Intimacy

Freud (1949) contended that the onset of sexual life is diphasic: beginning in infancy, interrupted during latency, and resumed at puberty. Eros (the love instinct), through its mobile libidinal energy, aims to establish ever-greater unities and to preserve them through organization and a coordination of the general pursuit of pleasure into the sexual function. Obtaining pleasure from erotogenic zones of the body is instinctual, and subsequently facilitates the reproductive function.

While no evidence of a displaceable sexual energy has been found, the concept that persons instinctively will pursue sexual gratification results in a belief by some that "the beast must be curbed." Consequently, prohibitive measures are deemed necessary in order to ensure the restriction of instinctual gratification. Often such prohibition takes the form of withholding information regarding sexual pleasure, normal reproductive physiology, and contraception in the belief that to do otherwise would inspire and facilitate the acting out of the sexual drive. Such a conviction does little to foster an individual's accurate sense of self and self-worth or to inculcate fundamentals of responsible sexual behavior.

Sullivan (1953) recognized the need for validation and acceptance manifested by the preadolescent: the pleasure desired through friendship with a "chum" and the experiencing of mutual concern and caring. He believed that the experience of loneliness reaches its full significance in the preadolescent era and that, because loneliness is "more terrible than anxiety," fear and anxiety do not inhibit the preadolescent from seeking to relieve it.

Sullivan (1953) also postulated three needs arising in adolescence: the need for personal security (freedom from anxiety), the need for intimacy (collaboration with at least one other), and the need for "lustful satisfaction" (sexual activity "in pursuit of the orgasm"). He contended that problems arise in "collisions" between these needs as the adolescent seeks to satisfy them, the most ubiquitous being the collision between the adolescent's motivation toward sexual activity and the security emerging through self-esteem and personal worth.

It follows that if one accepts concepts such as human instinctual drives, dynamisms, and naturally occurring needs that determine sexual behavior, one would seek to facilitate their expression in such a way that the adolescent achieves a satisfactory and fulfilling outcome. Strong infusions of guilt, like castor oil, can indeed regulate behavior in accordance with a desired end, but a guilt-dependent motivational system within the personality will mean a correspondingly inhibited development of one's sense of identity, emancipation, and self-worth. Instead, emphasis should be placed on facilitative interventions designed to enhance feelings of personal worth and acceptance of the emerging physical self. Providing accurate information regarding sexuality and fertility within such a context should enhance the prospect of responsible sexual behavior. Such a contention appears substantiated by research by Zelnik and Kantner (1973), who found a strong relationship between contraceptive use and self-perception among a national survey of 4,611 women 15 through 19 years of age. In an earlier survey (Goldsmith, Gabrielson, Gabrielson, Matthews, & Potts, 1972), findings suggested that an attitude of accepting one's own sexuality is a more important correlate with contraceptive use than knowledge of sex and contraception, religious background, or exposure to sex education.

The Learning of Sexual Behavior

> . . . learning about sex in our society is in large part learning about guilt; and learning how to manage sexuality commonly involves learning how to manage guilt. (Gagnon & Simon, 1970, p. 28)

Behavioral theory and research affords some insight in further understanding human sexuality and fertility. It has been suggested that children learn very little sexual behavior from their parents imitatively, since parents engage in very little public sex behavior. Yet it is believed that parents do transmit their conditioned emotional responses to sexual stimuli. A child inquiring about the reproductive process and sex differences is frequently responded to by parents who exhibit heightened anxiety, give nonhuman examples, present a minimum amount of information, or elect to postpone responding directly (Bandura & Walters, 1959; Sears, Macoby, & Levin, 1957). Modeling behavior is more likely to be provided by the peer group, older children, and the mass media (Bandura & Walters, 1963). Parental negative conditioning can result in an adolescent's fear that parents will learn of his or her initial sexual experiences. Guilt and anxiety are not far behind. The failure to provide examples of discriminative and adaptive sexual behavior can only result in misinformation. Adolescent pregnancy is not so surprising when we see such discontinuity and conflict between conditioning and cultural demands (Bandura & Walters, 1963).

A model of psychosexual development based on cognitive-social learning theory has been proposed that describes the acquiring of sexual scripts that "give the self, other persons, and situations erotic abilities or content" (Gagnon & Simon, 1970, p. 25; Gagnon & Simon, 1973). Preadolescent sexual behavior is seen as not directly related to sexual gratification or sexual feelings but rather the "use of sex for non-sexual goals and purposes" (Gagnon & Simon, 1970, p. 27). Learned values related to sex are believed to greatly influence children's own role performances and judgments in subsequent intimate relationships and sexual behavior.

The gaining of admiration, approval, and affection during the latency period depends upon achievement. Lack of this sense of achievement and the concomitant rewards can result in an enduring sense of inferiority (Erikson, 1959). Many of us can recall the significance of common "rites" that implicitly recognized sexual development: a pubescent girl's first bra, menarche, the first time she wore hose or makeup, or that first time the barber deftly applied warmed shaving cream to a pubescent boy's sideburns and trimmed them with a razor that had been honed on the leather strap. Today these rites seem to have paled in their symbolic significance as latency-age children are often inundated with objects traditionally viewed as having sexual significance. This is an example of social forces that sexualize the child during latency long before corresponding biological sexual development. The objects retain their socially prescribed sexual symbolism and thus are associated with values and behaviors normally beyond the discriminative, psychological, and physiological capacity of the latency-age child. Problems can arise if the child correlates possession of sexually symbolic objects with being sexual and attempts to garner affection, approval, and admiration through corresponding sexual achievements. Such a process can effectively eliminate latency as a distinct developmental phase, and inhibit the acquisition and development of important self-perceptions and abilities that facilitate one's subsequent sense of identity and capacity for intimacy with another.

A current trend in the commercial enterprise and marketing strategy of many companies that manufacture clothing and cosmetics is toward the use of young adolescent and preadolescent models. Typically the ads suggest that youthful sensuality (e.g., tight jeans covering a lively pelvis in combination with glossy lips swept slowly with the tip of the tongue) is rewarded with the head-snapping attention of the opposite sex. The possible modeling effect of this form of commercialism is something to be concerned about, especially considering the relative paucity of media portrayals of relationships based on trust, mutual admiration, understanding, and acceptance.

Other Influences on Adolescent Sexual Behavior

Research by Byrne (1977) has demonstrated that when sexual cues elicit negative feelings in an individual, that person is less likely to anticipate sexual behavior, acquire contraceptives, communicate accurately about birth control with the sex partner, or utilize contraceptive methods that require direct contact with the genitals, and consequently is more likely to risk an unwanted pregnancy. Other high-risk groups include those adolescent females whose parents' marriage is relatively hostile and the daughter sides with father against mother, or those who feel alienated from the mother and are experiencing a father-daughter relationship that is exclusive and quasisexual (Abernathy, 1976).

In a study by Jorgenson, King, and Torrey (1980), it was found that qualities of the adolescent sexual dyad such as relationship satisfaction and interpersonal power correlated more consistently with exposure to pregnancy risk than either family or peer relationships. Female power in the contraceptive and sexual components of the relationship was found to be inversely related to the risk of pregnancy. The stronger the female "voice," the less the risk. The use of contraceptives by peers and overall relationship satisfaction appeared to enhance the prospect of regular and effective contraceptive use.

Elkind (1967) has described two aspects of adolescent egocentrism that can influence adolescent sexual behavior: the "personal fable" (overdifferentiation of the uniqueness of one's affect and emotions) and "the imaginary audience" (a result of the adolescent's failure to differentiate thought objects). Consequently, the adolescent couple may believe that they cannot get pregnant ("I am special") and are reluctant to "announce" to themselves and their imaginary audience (parents, partner, peers, etc.) that they are willing to accept their sexuality, or otherwise consciously prepare themselves for sex by learning about or utilizing contraception. Thus, the adolescent's own egocentrism may be a primary factor of resistance in acknowledging the "facts of life" and dealing with sexuality in a responsible manner, despite efforts by parents or sex educators who emphasize the risks of pregnancy and explain reproductive physiology. The presence of the personal fable is believed to persist beyond that of the imaginary audience, and may extend into adulthood. Elkind (1967) contends that in general, however, the adolescent's egocentrism is effectively overcome through the establishment of close relationships with others, or what Erikson (1959) has termed "intimacy."

The adolescent's resistance in acknowledging the emergence of sexuality may be shared by parents. Indeed, a family crisis may occur as the adolescent's sexuality becomes manifest. The family system is stressed as the adolescent member undergoes a virtual physical and psychological metamorphosis. The parents may be reluctant to adapt to or otherwise acknowledge their child's struggle to establish an independent identity. Thus, it may be through sexual behavior or sex-role issues that the adolescent can assert independence. Often, family conflicts over dress or hair style, for example, may be symbolic of issues related to the adolescent's developing sexually. Under such circumstances, family communication and the trust among its members may be severely tested, and warrant remedial attention in order that the necessary changes within the family system can be realized and accepted by the family members. The goal is to facilitate open family discussion about sex and to enhance the prospect of effective and satisfying communication and trust.

Many adolescents (and adults) abstain from intercourse. Clearly, abstinence is the most effective means of birth control available to anyone. We have to bear in mind, however, that in some persons, celibacy may essentially preclude all sexual pleasure. It may represent a pervasive denial of one's own sexuality or result in the avoidance of any sort of intimacy with another. In such cases, the possibility of underlying issues must be recognized and explored. Abstinence may, however, be the responsible choice of one who is relatively self-aware and reflect such an individual's own personal values.

The therapist who attends to individuals, couples, and families who present problems related to adolescent sexuality needs to be cognizant of his or her own attitudes and values as well. Because the therapist has already experienced adolescence and perhaps many of the associated conflicts, he or she is vulnerable to the potential influence of "unfinished business" that is apt to interfere with the therapeutic process. The therapist's own unresolved issues can be projected onto the client system, or otherwise become manifest through transference and countertransference phenomena.

In addressing client's concerns, the therapist may be required to assume the roles of sex educator, advocate, or permission giver, or he or she may serve as a model for the client. This means that the therapist must feel comfortable in assuming roles beyond that of counselor. Effective performance of these therapeutic roles can facilitate the client's own informed and independent sense of self, from which fulfilling and responsible personal choices related to sexuality and fertility can emerge.

In summary, while additional research is needed in order to further determine the complex relationships between the multitude of variables that influence adolescent sexual behavior, the evidence to date suggests the importance of the quality of the adolescent's relationships with parents, peers, and intimates; the availability of accurate information regarding sexuality and fertility; the availability of contraceptives; modeling influences; and perhaps most significantly, the adolescent's awareness and acceptance of himself or herself as a sexual being capable of responsible sexual behavior.

MANAGING FERTILITY IN THE COMMITTED OR MARITAL RELATIONSHIP

Parenthood represents a developmental and transitional crisis (Hobbs, 1965; LeMasters, 1965). Invariably it involves role reorganization that must result in the couple's accommodation to the new family member while maintaining the bond of the marital or committed relationship. This process is facilitated by the couple's separating from and establishing new ways of connection with their families of origin, developing effective ways of communicating their wants and needs to each other, and working through the issues of separateness and connectedness, closeness and distance, and autonomy and responsibility in relation to each other (Golan, 1978; Scherz, 1971).

Managing fertility (sometimes referred to as family planning) is thus dependent upon managing the relationship as a whole. The individual's awareness, choice, knowledge, and responsibility alluded to earlier are equally important within the relationship, but these must be transformed to accommodate the inclusion of an intimate partner. At the same time, true intimacy with another, and the concomitant sense of satisfaction and pleasure, depend upon the maintenance of one's own sense of personal identity (Erikson, 1959).

An individual or couple can externalize responsibility with the attitude or expectation that the environment or fate or others determine behavior and overall level of satisfaction, or they can see their lives as resulting from their own choices. The couple who choose not to discuss fertility issues or share their associated expectations and mutually agree as to how to manage their fertility are simply refusing to make the implicit explicit: that they are by and large responsible for their choices—including the choice not to acknowledge this fact.

If So, How Many and When?

If a couple makes explicit their intention to manage their fertility, they are doing so in anticipation of an intended end: to postpone childbearing and parenthood for a given time for given reasons, to pursue becoming parents, to reduce or enhance the likelihood of an additional pregnancy if they are already parents, to indefinitely postpone parenthood, or not to have any, or any more, children. A multitude of factors may influence such considerations: attitude toward self, one's partner, and the relationship; career considerations; projected financial ability; and so on. It is important to note that responsible management of fertility is always characterized by present choices that signify individual or mutual intent.

A deliberate and powerful assertion of intent constitutes an expression of commitment and responsibility that may or may not be congruent with the attitudes and expectations of one's partner, friends, relatives, or the potential grandparents. The frequent result is pain, disappointment, frustration, and heightened ambivalence—at least for someone. It is important that agendas, like stray dogs, be returned to their rightful owner and, if necessary, attempts be made to assuage persistently frictional outcomes of differences through direct and effective communication in the hope of achieving a mutual sense of understanding and acceptance.

The attributes of complexity, rigidity, conventionality, and satisfaction within sexual scripts can be identified and utilized in comparing and clarifying discrepancies between ideal or desired scripts and "performative" scripts (Gagnon, Rosen, & Leiblum, 1982). As a result, an individual can become more aware of personal beliefs and expectations with regard to fertility as well as those of the partner. Therapeutic modification of the scripts is possible in order to reduce discrepancies between the fantasy ideal and actual behavior.

COPING WITH UNWANTED PREGNANCY

Recent studies (Hilliard, Shank, & Redman, 1982; Anderson, Morris, & Gesche, 1977; Weller, 1976) have determined that nearly one-half of all pregnancies ending in live births are unplanned. Eighty-six percent of the pregnancies among unmarried teens in 1978 were unintended, as were 51% of pregnancies among those who were married (Alan Guttmacher Institute, 1981). One recent study determined that unplanned pregnancies constituted 40 to 50% of pregnancies resulting in live births among higher income, more educated, and older groups within the sample population (Hilliard, et al., 1982). Clearly a significant proportion of pregnancies are unplanned or unintended.

An unplanned pregnancy does not necessarily constitute an unwanted pregnancy. At some level, pregnancy may be desired but not accordingly planned for. For example, the individual or couple may suppress the desire to become pregnant to the extent that it becomes a hidden agenda for one or both partners and the pregnancy is subsequently viewed as unintentional.

In any case, there are only two alternatives when pregnancy is confirmed: to continue or to terminate it. If the first alternative is chosen, a decision must be made in some cases whether to keep the baby or give it up for adoption. Important to note is the fact that regardless of what decision is made the pregnancy may or may not be wanted. This distinction is not necessarily dependent upon the decision to terminate or continue the pregnancy, and vice versa. Psychological adjustment to pregnancy and its outcome would seem to depend heavily upon the congruence of various factors.

Some Important Legal Considerations

Current philosophical, theological, political, and public debate as to whether women should be able to choose to procure abortions or carry their pregnancies to term is exceedingly emotional and complex. There is ample opportunity for confusion on the part of both counselor and client alike. Thus, it is important to recount some important aspects of U.S. Supreme Court decisions that have implications in those counseling situations where abortion is considered as a means of coping with unwanted pregnancy.

In *Roe v. Wade,** the U.S. Supreme Court declared that during the first trimester of pregnancy (at least, depending on individual state statutes), women had a virtually unqualified right to abortion. This was based on the constitutionally guaranteed right to privacy, which was seen as entitling women to make choices affecting their own bodies without undue interference from the state.

The case of *Planned Parenthood of Central Missouri v. Danforth*** resulted in the determination that the mother's rights are held to be paramount and that the father should not have a right to veto a decision made by the mother. The court rejected any requirement for consent by the father of the fetus, by the spouse of the mother, or by the parents of the mother if she is an unmarried minor (at least during the first trimester of pregnancy).

The therapist should, of course, also be cognizant of the legal requirements of the individual state, the agency policy with regard to abortion counseling, if he or she has such affiliation, and various legal considerations pertinent to adoption as well.

Choosing How To Cope

The client who faces decisions about coping with an unwanted pregnancy is best served by the therapist who adopts a supportive role that facilitates the

---

*410 U.S. 113 (1973)
**428 U.S. 52 (1976)

client's own choosing. This orientation is enhanced by the counselor's nonjudgmental attitude and his or her awareness of relevant resources and alternatives. The possible outcomes associated with each alternative may need to be evaluated according to the influences of such mitigating factors as the nature of the client's support system, physical and psychological health, and the quality of relationships with significant others. Of course, this must be done within a time frame mediated by the extent of pregnancy since some alternatives have limited availability.

The therapist must be prepared to extend supportive interventions beyond the point of the client's making a decision, or arrange for continuity of support through other resources. For many clients, making an explicit decision about one's intent is a most arduous task. Responsibility often weighs heavy, especially when having to choose how to deal with an unwanted pregnancy in today's society. As in other crisis situations, the therapist may be denied the opportunity for follow-up, since he or she may be associated with the uncomfortable thoughts and feelings experienced during the crisis by the individual, couple, or family, who effectively deny the therapist "psychological access" after the crisis has passed.

Counseling with clients who present with an unplanned, unintended, or unwanted pregnancy affords the opportunity to further explore their attitudes toward their own sexuality and fertility and their options for a more effective and satisfying means of managing fertility. A successful, adaptive response to the situation can be growth producing and serve as a model for facilitating future awareness, choice, and responsibility.

ISSUES CONCERNING INFERTILITY

It has been estimated that 5 to 10% of couples experience habitual and repeated spontaneous abortion or miscarriage and that 10 to 15% of American married couples cannot conceive (Roland, 1968). Through thorough testing, a medical diagnosis can be established in approximately 80% of these cases. About 30% of the time the male's infertility is established, whereas in about 50% of the cases the problem is attributed to the female. The remaining 20% of diagnosed cases reveal the infertility to be the result of the problems of both partners (Mazer, 1979).

Infertility is seen as a developmental crisis for those persons who wish to conceive (Kraft, Palombo, Mitchell, Dean, Meyers, & Schmidt, 1980) as it may require the assessment and adaptive resolution of disturbances of body image, attitudes toward parenthood, and dealing with "the grief and pain of missing out forever on a basic life experience that had been tacitly anticipated'' (p. 623).

Choices pertinent to how an individual or couple manages their infertility become paramount. The loss of the capacity to have choices regarding fertility may be compensated for through recognizing how one may choose to act in light of such loss. It is important to ascertain the meaning that the loss of the ability to conceive has to the individual and the partner, and to determine their subjective experience and what it implies about themselves and their relationship. If perceptions of the self or the relationship are deleterious, this topic must be addressed since it may determine, at least to a significant extent, compensatory decisions the individual or couple may make in response to their infertility. It has been suggested (Kraft et al., 1980), for example, that the successful adoption of a child by an infertile couple may depend on the resolution of such perceptions.

In the absence of procreative capacity, sexuality may assume new meaning for the individual or couple. One or both partners may withdraw sexually, with the effect of denying themselves pleasure. Or, one may seek compensatory solace in sexually promiscuous behavior. A dysfunctional sexual reaction is possible, especially for those individuals or couples whose sexual identity is primarily linked to their procreative capacity.

Adjustment reactions may be particularly severe in those infertile couples or individuals for whom a medical diagnosis has not been established. In the absence of a definitive explanation, they may, at some level, create and assume an erroneous one that has profoundly negative effects with respect to perception of self or of the partner and the relationship.

In the course of a medical work-up for infertility, the couple may resort to having sexual intercourse ''on schedule,'' for example, as dictated by a variation in the woman's basal body temperature. It would seem important, for both individuals and their relationship, that sexual intercourse not become devoid of pleasure. While sex on schedule may be necessary medically or diagnostically, it is equally important that the couple maintain, and even seek to enhance, their mutual communication, caring, and concern for each other during this potentially difficult period. Indeed, reviewing a commitment to mutual sexual pleasure may be an effective means of coping with infertility or those cases where conception is difficult.

Additional persons at risk are those who have postponed attempting to become biological parents for various reasons, for example, career considerations, and presume the ability to conceive but choose to wait. If the perceived deadline is not met, they may experience additional stress because of the fear that ''time is running out.''

It is clearly evident that issues relating to infertility are dependent upon the particular meaning the condition has for the individual and his or her partner, and that the couple's psychological adjustment is primarily dependent upon their ability to "work through" these issues. Professional therapeutic intervention must address these perceptions and facilitate compensatory attitudes and behaviors that are satisfying and otherwise productive. Considered alternatives to biological parenthood, such as adoption or the decision to have no children, ideally demand the same degree of awareness, knowledge, and responsibility that would be required in the absence of infertility.

THE DECISION TO HAVE NO CHILDREN

Approximately 5% of couples voluntarily decide not to have children (Veevers, 1972a). In foregoing parenthood, these couples are not acceding to the values of the dominant culture that couples ought to want to have children, and that they should have children.

A study by Veevers (1973) revealed two distinct and characteristic ways in which couples are voluntarily childless. In the first of these (approximately one-third of the sample population), the couple decides explicitly and prior to marriage not to pursue parenthood. In the second, childbearing is postponed in a series of decisions until the couple decides once and for all not to have any children.

Voluntarily childless women are subject to the possibility of negative stereotyping, for example, being described as abnormal, nonfeminine, selfish, unhappy, immature, unfulfilled, and irresponsible (Veevers, 1972b). However, most of the women in the study cited in the preceding paragraph were found to be well-defended against the potential impact of negative reactions to their choice, and experienced a sense of reaffirmation and support through their partner's consensual validation.

Therapeutic intervention may indeed be warranted when partners have disparate convictions in regard to having or not having children. In these instances, if not most, the couple will likely decide not to marry if one or both are adamant, as such divergence constitutes a serious difference. This may be, in part at least, why many couples seem loath to explicitly discuss their mutual hopes and expectations related to childbearing prior to marriage, that is, for fear of relationship-threatening differences and their possible present and future implications. Regardless of whether the couple is married or not, however, the difference must be explored and its validity assessed as it may be indicative of the presence of underlying and unacknowledged issues within the individuals and/or the relationship itself.

The consensual agreement between partners not to have any children necessitates, of course, that the couple agree to effectively and consistently manage their fertility if they are capable of conceiving. They must also surrender definitive associations between their sense of sexual identity and self-worth and the roles associated with parenthood.

SUMMARY

Because of the general lack of agreement in today's society as to the appropriate forms of pleasure-oriented and procreative sexual behavior, individuals and couples are subject to confusing messages from social institutions, the media, significant others, etc. This indicates a necessity for the individual, couple, or family to acquire the accurate knowledge, self-awareness, and freedom to responsibly determine their needs, wants, and expectations with regard to how they manage their fertility. Such a process, while potentially difficult and anxiety provoking, can be facilitated by the helping professional who possesses a knowledge of the reproductive process, the various forms of contraception, and the variety of alternatives available to the person or couple who presents with a fertility-related problem. The family therapist must have knowledge of the myriad potential issues surrounding the topics of adolescent sexuality, managing fertility in the marital or committed relationship, unwanted pregnancy, infertility, and the decision to have no children. With effective guidance, he or she can help such persons to establish, reestablish, or maintain a healthy self-concept and sexual identity, which are vital to a fulfilling and satisfying life.

REFERENCES

Abernathy, V. Prevention of unwanted pregnancy among teenagers. *Primary Care*, 1976, *3*, 399-406.

The Alan Guttmacher Institute. *Teenage pregnancy: The problem that hasn't gone away*. New York: The Alan Guttmacher Institute, 1981.

Anderson, J.E., Morris, L., & Gesche, M. Planned and unplanned fertility in upstate New York. *Family Planning Perspectives*, 1977, *9*, 4-11.

Bandura, A., & Walters, R.H. *Adolescent aggression*. New York: Ronald, 1959.

Bandura, A., & Walters, R.H. *Social learning and personality development*. New York: Holt, Rinehart & Winston, 1963.

Byrne, D. A pregnant pause in the sexual revolution. *Psychology Today*, July 1977, pp. 67-68.

Elkind, D. Egocentrism in adolescence. *Child Development*, 1967, *38*, 1025-1034.

Erikson, E. Growth and crises of the healthy personality. *Psychological Issues*, 1959, *1*, 50-100.

Freud, S. [*An outline of psychoanalysis*]. (J. Strachey, Trans.). New York: Norton, 1949.

Gagnon, J.H., Rosen, R.C., & Leiblum, S.R. Cognitive and social aspects of sexual dysfunction: Sexual scripts in sex therapy. *Journal of Sex and Marital Therapy*, 1982, *8*, 44-56.

Gagnon, J.H., & Simon, W. Psychosexual development. In J.H. Gagnon & W. Simon (Eds.), *The sexual scene*. Chicago: Aldine, 1970.

Gagnon, J.H., & Simon, W. *Sexual conduct: The social sources of human sexuality*. Chicago: Aldine, 1973.

Golan, N. *Treatment in crisis situations*. New York: Free Press, 1978.

Goldsmith, S., Gabrielson, M.O., Gabrielson, I., Matthews, V., & Potts, L. Teenagers, sex and contraception. *Family Planning Perspectives*, 1972, *4*, 32-38.

Hilliard, D., Shank, J.C., & Redman, R.W. Unplanned pregnancies in a midwestern community. *The Journal of Family Practice*, 1982, *15*, 259-263.

Hobbs, D. Parenthood as a crisis: A third study. *Journal of Marriage and the Family*, 1965, *27*, 367-372.

Jorgensen, S., King, S., & Torrey, B. Dyadic and social network influences on adolescent exposure to pregnancy risk. *Journal of Marriage and the Family*, 1980, *42*, 141-155.

Kraft, A., Palombo, J., Mitchell, D., Dean, C., Meyers, S., & Schmidt, A.W. The psychological dimensions of infertility. *American Journal of Orthopsychiatry*, 1980, *50*, 618-628.

LeMasters, E.E. Parenthood as crisis. In H. Parad (Ed.), *Crisis intervention: Selected readings*. New York: Family Service Association of America, 1965.

Mazer, M. Barren couples. *Psychology Today*, May 1979, pp. 101-112.

Montagu, A. *Sex, man and society*. New York: G.P. Putnam, 1969.

Roland, J. Management of the infertile couple. Springfield, Ill.: Charles C Thomas, 1968.

Scherz, F.H. Maturational crises and parent-child interaction. *Social Casework*, 1971, *52*, 362-369.

Sears, R.R., Macoby, E.E., & Levin, H. *Patterns of child rearing*. New York: Harper, 1957.

Sullivan, H.S. *The interpersonal theory of psychiatry*. New York: Norton, 1953.

U.S. Reports. Vol. 410. Washington, D.C.: U.S. Government Printing Office, 1973.

U.S. Reports. Vol. 428. Washington, D.C.: U.S. Government Printing Office, 1976.

Veevers, J.E. Factors in the incidence of childlessness in Canada: An analysis of census data. *Social Biology*, 1972, *19*, 266-274. (a)

Veevers, J.E. The violation of fertility mores: Voluntary childlessness as deviant behavior. In C.L. Boydell, C.F. Grindstaff, & P.C. Whitehead (Eds.), *Deviant behavior and societal reaction*. Toronto: Holt, Rinehart & Winston, 1972. (b)

Veevers, J.E. Voluntarily childless wives. *Sociology and Social Research*, 1973, *57*, 356-366.

Weller, R.H. Number and timing failures among legitimate births in the United States: 1968, 1969, 1972. *Family Planning Perspectives*, 1976, *8*, 111-116.

Zelnik, M., & Kantner, J.F. Contraception and pregnancy: Experiences of young unmarried women in the United States. *Family Planning Perspectives*, 1973, *5*, 21-35.

Zelnik, M., & Kanter, J.F. Reasons for nonuse of contraception by sexually active women aged 15-19. *Family Planning Perspectives*, 1979, *11*, 289-296.

3. Sexual Disorders and the Family Therapist

Collier M. Cole, PhD
Clinical Assistant Professor
Department of Psychiatry and
  Behavioral Sciences
The University of Texas Medical Branch
  at Galveston
Galveston, Texas

It is increasingly common today for family therapists to encounter and uncover sexual problems when working with clients in treatment. This typically comes about either directly, with couples presenting this area as a chief complaint, or indirectly, where the real sexual concern arises after one or more preliminary issues are discussed. Harold Lief, M.D. (1982), a pioneer in the area of marital and sex therapies, recently noted that "It's impossible to do sex therapy without dealing with the nature of the couple's relationship" (p. 3). This observation has certainly been substantiated in the clinical and research endeavors of many professionals.

Sex counseling requires much more than simply presenting explicit audio-visual materials and assigning homework activities that involve increasingly intimate tasks for a couple to perform. Not only must a therapist have knowledge regarding basic issues in sexuality and specific techniques to initiate change, but he or she must also be able to communicate this information in an articulate, sensitive, and appropriate fashion based upon each couple's unique needs and problems. And, as with any successful therapeutic intervention, one must have a solid grasp of the dynamics of the situation in order for specific techniques to be effective in promoting change.

The present article is designed to explore some of the most common sexual problems that family therapists are likely to encounter. These problems, as well as causal factors, will be described and suggestions will be offered for working with couples where sexual concerns are presented as a chief complaint. Specifically, a set of guidelines or principles for maximizing sexual pleasure and satisfaction will be presented.

ETIOLOGY

Crooks and Baur (1980) outlined four general areas involved in the development of sexual problems. *Cultural factors* refer to those influences that are likely to affect all of us who grow up in Western society, though the impact may vary from one family to another or from one culture to another. These include the "double standard," which suggests that men may behave in one sexual fashion while women must adhere to a different set of rules. For example, men must be experts and the initiators of activity and are always ready for sex. Women should be passive and accept their duty, though a good woman really should not enjoy sex too much. Similarly, the goal-specific notion that real sex involves penis-vagina intercourse, and only this activity, can set the stage for many problems.

Personal factors refer to the unique and complex elements in each individual that can shape sexual attitudes and behaviors (e.g., the presence or absence of adequate sex information and education, a positive versus a negative self-concept, the presence or absence of emotional problems or identifiable mental disorders). Negative childhood learning experiences (e.g., incest, rape, punishment for genital exploration and masturbation) are also capable of influencing one's view of sexual activity in adulthood.

Interpersonal factors that can affect sexual functioning include ineffective sexual communication styles (e.g., not openly discussing sexual needs or desires, making assumptions about what one should or should not be doing sexually), discord in other areas of the relationship (e.g., financial, parental, vocational), fears about pregnancy, and problems related to sexual orientation (e.g., one partner may be struggling with issues of homosexuality, transsexualism, or transvestism).

Finally, there exists a number of *organic factors* that can affect sexual functioning, although most sexologists agree that these variables are responsible for only about 10% of sexual problems. It is of interest to note, however, that most couples seeking sex counseling initially attribute their difficulties to some medical cause. Often a thorough medical evaluation plus supportive comments from the counselor ("This does not mean you are crazy or have a mental disorder causing this problem") are required before the couple will begin to consider the psychosocial components that are contributing to the situation. Some of the specific organic factors that can affect sexual performance and satisfaction include: illnesses (e.g., multiple sclerosis, diabetes, brain tumors, severe arthritis, lower back problems, endocrine diseases, spinal cord injury), medications (e.g., anticholinergic drugs, antihypertensive drugs, psychotropic medications, birth control pills), and a variety of conditions resulting in painful intercourse experiences for both men and women (e.g., infections of the genital organs, Peyronies disease in men, endometriosis in women).

In practice, as a therapist interviews a couple with sexual difficulties, it is usually discovered that a blend of the first three factors has contributed to the development of the problem. For example, a classic case summary might include the following: "Both partners grew up in environments where sex was not discussed or was viewed as dirty; issues involving the double standard are present and certain types of sexual activity are considered unacceptable; both partners are feeling low regard for each other as well as deflated self-confidence; and the interpersonal relationship has suffered to some extent as a result of the situation (e.g., feelings of apathy or hopelessness, decreased communication regarding sexual matters and perhaps other areas of their relationships as well)."

It is unclear at present why certain couples who are experiencing sexual difficulties identify the situation as a problem. Frank, Anderson, and Rubinstein (1978) studied 100 "happy" couples who had never sought sex counseling and who described their marital relationship as being free of significant distress. Although over 80% of these couples reported their sexual relations to be happy and satisfying, a significant percentage of the men and women interviewed reported periodic difficulties ranging from lack of interest or inability to relax to ejaculatory, erectile, and orgasmic problems. What is of interest is the fact that most of these couples appeared to accept the temporary, transitory nature of the situation (indeed, all men and women experience periodic episodes where sexual performance and satisfaction fall below their customary average) and did not focus on a problem that needed to be addressed or fixed. Similarly, Cole, Blakeney, Chan, Chesney, and Creson's (1979) investigation of couples who had requested sex counseling discovered little difference between symptomatic partners (who identified themselves as having a specific erectile or orgasmic problem) and asymptomatic partners with respect to early background and personality variables. Specifically, such factors as parental-familial background, sexual attitudes and knowledge, and marital histories were compared for individuals diagnosed as symptomatic and their partners who received no sexual diagnosis. This suggests that most of us are exposed to the same sorts of experiences (cultural, personal, interpersonal) that can predispose us to encounter periodic sexual difficulties, yet only certain couples are likely to identify the situation as problematic. While the causal factors previously described may set the stage for later difficulties, there must be some additional factors that result in the situation leading to the therapist's office.

One possibility in this regard may be the classic notions of the "spectator role" and "fear of performance" (Masters & Johnson, 1970; Masters, Johnson, & Kolodny, 1982). Indeed, regardless of the variety or blend of causal factors that may initially predispose a couple to experience sexual difficulties, most sex counselors invariably can attribute persisting problems to a couple's being afraid to engage in sexual activity because of anticipated failure (i.e., fear of performance) and/or because they try to watch or grade themselves or their partner during sexual relations (i.e., spectator role). The desire to perform an intimate sexual act within a valued social context (i.e., marriage or an important relationship) can create feelings of tremendous pressure on an individual experiencing doubt about his or her sexual functioning. A pertinent analogy is the person who comes home late and fatigued and must go to sleep because he or she must be up early the next morning. The harder the person tries to fall asleep, often consciously scanning himself or herself for signs of impending drowsiness, the more difficult it becomes to achieve the goal. Sexually speaking, the more determined a person is to have an erection this time or to achieve climax this time, the more impossible it becomes, with the result being continued frustration and feelings of low self-esteem and low relationship regard. It is often important (as will be discussed later) for counseling intervention to focus on these immediate, here-and-now issues (i.e., fear of performance, the spectator role) in order to allow couples to begin experiencing more positive sexual feelings in the absence of blame, so that increased sexual satisfaction can be achieved. Treatment can quickly bog down if attention is exclusively focused on a discussion of past issues.

CLASSIFICATION OF SEXUAL PROBLEMS

The most common types of sexual problems likely to be encountered by the family therapists are outlined in the classification of psychosexual disorders in the American Psychiatric Association's *Diagnostic and Statistical Manual of Mental Disorders–Third Edition (DSM-III)* (1980). *Inhibited sexual desire* is a problem increasingly seen today by counselors. It can occur not only in relationships of long duration, but in relationships that have lasted for only a short time as well. One or both partners typically report little desire or interest in sexual activity. This problem often lasts for weeks or months and generally does not result from hormonal imbalances, but rather from psychosocial factors (e.g., apathy toward the relationship in general, a repertoire of sexual activity that is perceived as boring and repetitive, an absence of spontaneity and creativity in attending to one another sexually or nonsexually).

Inhibited sexual excitement refers to difficulties that are encountered specifically during the phase of sexual excitation. In males, this is generally manifested by problems in achieving or maintaining an erection sufficient for sexual activity (e.g., intercourse, masturbation). Most commonly, the problem is of a secondary nature. That is, the man has achieved satisfactory erections in the past (either with the current or a previous partner) but is unable to do so at the present time. The primary form of this problem, in which the man has never experienced an erection during sexual excitement, is a much rarer disorder. In females, inhibited sexual excitement refers to a partial or complete failure to attain and maintain the lubrication-swelling response typically associated with high sexual arousal. Again the problem may be of a primary or secondary nature, although the latter is more often encountered by the counselor.

Inhibited female orgasm describes a situation in which the individual is unable to experience climax following a normal sexual excitement phase. It is not at all uncommon to encounter this problem in its primary form, as many women in our culture grow up with limited sex information and the experience and attitude that sexual activity is a ''duty'' and should not be enjoyed. More often, however, the problem will be encountered in its secondary form, in which the woman has experienced orgasm in the past (either with the current or a previous partner) but is unable to achieve climax at the present time.

Inhibited male orgasm is a condition in which the man is unable to experience ejaculation and orgasm following an adequate phase of sexual excitement, and may occur in primary or secondary forms. One will often uncover feelings of low self-esteem or partner regard, fears about pregnancy, or discomfort with ''letting go'' in a sexual situation as contributors to this problem.

Premature ejaculation is a commonly encountered problem in which there is an inability to delay ejaculation despite a conscious effort on the part of the individual to do so. Generally, ejaculation will occur within a matter of seconds or a few minutes at most following sexual excitement. The problem can be most disturbing to a couple when intercourse is attempted and ejaculation rapidly occurs.

Functional dyspareunia can appear in both men or women and describes a condition in which sexual activity, particularly intercourse, results in recurrent and persistent genital pain and discomfort. It is generally recognized that psychosocial factors (as described earlier in this chapter) play a major etiological role in this problem, rather than organic factors.

Finally, *functional vaginismus* is characterized by a recurrent or persistent spasm of the musculature of the outer third of the vagina that directly interferes with sexual satisfaction and performance. It is usually impossible for penetration of the vagina to occur, either by the penis or any other object, resulting in much frustration on the part of both partners involved.

While the preceding classification of sexual disorders is geared toward individual problems, it is important to remember that sexual activity typically involves a dyadic encounter. This would suggest that even if one partner is identified as having a specific problem in the sexual area, the situation will have a significant impact on the other partner as well. In some cases, the impact may have a direct result on the other person's sexual functioning. For example, a man experiencing difficulties with prematurity or erectile problems often will have a female partner who is experiencing problems with being able to achieve orgasm through intercourse. This illustrates very clearly why it is critical to involve both partners in any type of sexual counseling intervention.

COUNSELING GUIDELINES FOR ENHANCING A SEXUAL RELATIONSHIP

Most experts would agree that sexual arousal is a normal biological response that occurs in the presence of certain kinds of stimulation and psychoenvironmental factors. From a counseling standpoint, therefore, it is impossible to teach someone how to have this biological response or how to will an orgasm. The kinds of difficulties that couples encounter in this area can be accounted for by a variety and combination of roadblocks (i.e., etiological factors noted previously) that inhibit or interfere with the normal response pattern. In addition, feelings of anxiety regarding sexual contact (e.g., fear of performance) will further exacerbate the situation. Counseling, therefore, should focus on helping couples to reduce or remove these roadblocks in order to facilitate satisfactory sexual intimacy.

In many cases, the family therapist who discovers that a couple is having sexual problems is in a unique position to be able to initiate change. It is very likely that significant improvement can be made by helping a couple to relearn and reexperience more satisfying ways to communicate with respect to sexual matters. Regardless of the specific etiological factors involved and the partners' individual views of the situation, it is possible to influence their relationship by encouraging them to rethink some of their attitudes and ideas regarding sexuality.

The following guidelines or principles for enhancing a sexual relationship have been developed within a clinical format to aid couples experiencing sexual difficulties. They are reprinted with the permission of the Galveston-based Marital-Sexual Enrichment Program, which has been working with couples for more than 10 years using a weekend workshop approach (Blakeney, Kinder, Creson, Powell, & Sutton, 1976; Cole, Chan, Blakeney, & Chesney, 1980; Powell, Blakeney, & Croft, 1974). Couples check into a Galveston hotel for two and a half days and are presented during this time with sex education information through teaching and films, specific sexual assignments to experience in the privacy of their own room (e.g., sensate focus exercises), and individualized couple-oriented counseling with respect to their own unique problems and concerns.

One of the most important elements of this program is the individualized dyadic counseling. Specifically, the key strategy employed is the presentation and discussion of the set of guidelines for enhancing a sexual relationship. These principles were developed by the Galveston treatment team as a result of discovering that a majority of couples' sexual complaints were being perpetuated by their current attitudes regarding sexual functioning and the ways in which they responded to one another concerning sexual matters (i.e., the sexual communication process). A review of these guidelines will be helpful in understanding the common complaints encountered and ways in which a counselor can intervene.

1. *The goal of sexual activity is that you leave each encounter feeling better about yourself and your partner. This is the only endpoint and says nothing about climax or orgasm. Do not ask for orgasm.* This principle strikes at the core of the problem for many couples who perceive penis-vagina intercourse as the only form of real sex. Unless each encounter ends with intercourse and orgasm the experience is often discounted as being unsatisfactory. It is important for couples to realize and give up this self-defeating and narrow goal in order to experience and appreciate other satisfying sexual behaviors.

2. *Giving is pleasurable and can be enjoyed, but should be on a non-demand basis. Ask only that your partner receive your gift.* The notion of partners' assuming giving and receiving roles during a sexual encounter is vital in developing satisfying sex relations. Too often a couple may believe that one partner is supposed to be the initiator or giver during an activity, and by so doing will receive something in return. Or, the other partner may begin to feel that he or she is placing too great a demand on the giver, who certainly cannot be enjoying the situation. These fixed notions can be very detrimental to achieving a satisfying sexual relationship.

3. *Learn to receive pleasure without feeling obligated to give. By enjoying the gift of your partner, you are in fact giving pleasure.* The idea behind this guideline is very similar to the preceding one. Couples need to be more aware that giving and receiving roles are mutually enjoyable, can be alternated through a simple verbal request, and are not fixed states that they are locked into for each subsequent sexual encounter.

4. *Sex involves a continuum of activity, and not just intercourse. Sexuality and sensuality are intimately related. Sensuality includes touching, smelling, tasting, hearing, and seeing.* Clinically speaking, most couples

struggling with sexual concerns are focusing their attention on a problem with intercourse. In the process of trying to deal with the problem they have likely forgotten and neglected many of the other kinds of activities that can be sexually pleasurable and arousing (e.g., kissing, touching, caressing, holding hands, snuggling in bed). It can be very important for couples to reexperience these pleasurable activities, thus maintaining closeness and a positive atmosphere within the relationship as they continue to focus on their specific concerns. Further, it should be noted that sexuality and sensuality involve all five senses—and not the sixth sense, mind reading. The only way to be certain that the partner enjoys a particular sensation or activity, or would like to have the partner perform a specific activity, is to communicate verbally about the situation. Even in relationships of long duration, there is no guarantee that one can accurately predict or assume what the other person is thinking, feeling, or wanting. To do so suggests incorrectly that people's desires, attitudes, and values do not change over time. This particular guideline can be most difficult for couples to follow, because it requires taking a risk to share important personal feelings regarding sexuality, and doing so is usually an activity in which most couples in our society have little experience.

5. *Sex is an interaction between two individuals requiring clear communication and willing cooperation. Hear what your partner says without feeling criticized.* There is probably no other area within our personal lives about which we are more sensitive than the area of sexuality. Partners tend to be extremely careful in making comments to each other regarding sexual matters and often refrain from doing so out of fear of what the other person may say or do. It is therefore important for the counselor to point out that this kind of discussion is normal, positive, and can take place in such a way that both will experience satisfaction. The way to do this is to emphasize that such discussions are for the purpose of information, to learn more about each partner's likes, desires, and wants, rather than for the purposes of criticizing or blaming. (One additional observation—removing the word "sex" from the beginning of this particular guideline and replacing it with "marriage" or "relationship" will clearly show how intimately interwoven sex counseling is with a couple's overall relationship.)

6. *Learn to say yes instead of no. Give alternatives. Break the rejection cycle.* Sexual satisfaction and communication can be enhanced by teaching couples to use the "I language." Specifically, learning to start statements with "I" (e.g., "I feel . . .," "I like . . .," "I want . . ."), instead of "you" (e.g., "You feel . . .," "You want . . ."), increases the prob-

ability that the individual will have his or her message heard without the partner becoming defensive or feeling criticized. In other words, there is a greater likelihood for increased closeness and positive change to occur. For example, in a given situation, partners can learn to say "yes" instead of "no" to particular sexual activities. One may not be interested in intercourse, but could offer an alternative to the other person (e.g., "Dear, I don't feel like intercourse tonight, but I sure would like to snuggle with you."). This approach would lessen feelings of hurt and rejection and actually enhance closeness. One would be saying "no" to a particular activity but "yes" to the relationship.

7. *More enjoyable sex is better than increased quantity of sex. Enjoyable activity is self-reinforcing.* Couples are usually not aware that there are no fixed frequency rates for sexual activity. Often they present themselves initially as being concerned that there is too little or too much sexual activity occurring. The emphasis should be placed on increasing the quality of each sexual episode, rather than striving for some magical number of sexual encounters. Certainly any activity that is enjoyable, including sexual play, will be self-reinforcing and is likely to occur again.

8. *Sex should be fun and not work. Enjoyable sex requires interesting and interested partners.* One underemphasized factor that is most important for satisfying sexual relations is humor. Too frequently couples approach a sexual encounter, particularly when they have experienced problems in the past, with the attitude that they "must" or "should" perform perfectly, resulting in a situation that becomes work and is likely to be unsatisfying. Since human beings come in all shapes and sizes and conditions (i.e., there are individual differences with respect to body size, length of arms and legs, tolerance for fatigue, alcohol consumption, and so on), partners should be cautioned that sex is normally an awkward experience, one in which there are many opportunities to be less than perfect. Accordingly, it is helpful to encourage couples to maintain a sense of humor and to approach each episode with an attitude that the experience will be fun rather than work.

9. *Closeness may, at times, be too much, and either partner may need distance. It is important to learn to ask for distance without showing abandonment. Give reassurance to your partner that you will return.* The process of examining one's sexual relationship and experimenting with new thoughts and behaviors can be distressing and bring to the surface a variety of fears (e.g., feelings of low self-worth, inadequacy, fears of losing one's partner). This is a common and normal reaction. It is best to allow the person

experiencing such concerns some time to reflect and think through these issues, either individually or with counseling support. Using the "I language" as described above can be most helpful in openly and realistically communicating one's fears or doubts to a partner. Also, in order to decrease feelings of rejection or abandonment, it is beneficial to assure one's partner that the individual will resume the discussion at a later time.

10. *Go slowly, and give plenty of reassurance as needed.* This final guideline is perhaps the most important one and undoubtedly will need to be emphasized repeatedly. The basic truth is that it often requires time and much reassurance between partners before change and increasing satisfaction can occur and persist within the sexual relationship. Couples must approach each encounter as an opportunity for mutual fun, pleasure, and relationship growth, rather than a test to see if they can solve a problem. It is useful to point this out, as well as to emphasize that there will be innumerable opportunities for sexual experimentation in the future. If one particular encounter is less than satisfactory (a normal outcome that most individuals periodically experience at different times throughout their lives, as noted previously), the situation should be simply accepted as such, while realizing that there will be many other opportunities to improve and increase sexual satisfaction.

To review, the preceding principles can be a valuable treatment aid to the family therapist working with a couple expressing sexual concerns. First of all, these guidelines touch on virtually all of the key areas that are involved in the development and maintenance of sexual problems. Clinical experience suggests that most couples seeking help have difficulties with several of the areas discussed. Second, these guidelines can provide the therapist with specific and pertinent topics to be explored during counseling. Indeed, the fact that such principles exist can communicate a sense of normalcy to a couple and reassure them that the sorts of problems they are encountering are, for the most part, commonly shared by others. It is then more likely that a couple, in the presence of a supportive therapist who models verbally and nonverbally that sexual discussions are acceptable and healthy (i.e., "gives permission"), will share and question their previous attitudes and behaviors regarding sexual issues. Finally, it is beneficial to provide a couple with a printed copy of these principles for future references. (It is not unusual at all for couples to report on follow-up that they continue to refer to and discuss these guidelines, not only with respect to their sexual life but to their overall relationship as well.)

CONCLUSION

The family therapist is in an excellent position to deal with sexual problems. He or she may have already worked with the family unit on some other difficulties (e.g., parenting roles, vocational roles), thus establishing rapport and a working relationship that can facilitate a discussion of sexual concerns. In the event that this is the initial complaint, a sensitive therapist can still provide a sense of security and "okayness" to explore sexual concerns. What is most important, however, is for each therapist to realize that he or she is a human being first and thus subject to the same sorts of growing-up experiences and attitudes toward sexuality that a couple may hold. Accordingly, it is critical that each therapist be accepting of his or her own sexuality, as well as others' views and sexual practices, in order to be an effective change agent for a couple seeking help.

With the aid of the previously described guidelines for enhancing a sexual relationship, the basic goal in counseling couples with sexual concerns is to deemphasize performance and increase feelings of pleasure and relaxation. Regardless of the type of sexual problem the therapist encounters, it is possible to make substantial progress in helping couples achieve more satisfaction from sexual activity by helping them to reexamine their attitudes and communication style in this area. In the event that a couple's situation is complicated by problems with alcohol, drugs, or major mental disorders, a referral or consultation with a sex therapist may be warranted. In addition, it is always prudent to recommend a physical examination when medical factors are suspected as having an impact on the situation.

Sexual satisfaction is intimately interwoven within the fabric of the family unit, and helping a couple enhance and improve their sexual lives can have a tremendous positive impact on the entire family system (Witkin, 1977). In an atmosphere of caring and cooperation between couples and therapist, significant improvement can be realized.

REFERENCES

American Psychiatric Association. *Diagnostic and statistical manual of mental disorders* (3rd ed.). Washington, D.C.: Author, 1980.

Blakeney, P., Kinder, B., Creson, D., Powell, L., & Sutton, C. A short-term intensive workshop approach for the treatment of human sexual inadequacy. *Journal of Sex and Marital Therapy,* 1976, 2(2), 124-129.

Cole, C., Blakeney, P., Chan, F., Chesney, A., & Creson, D. The myth of symptomatic versus asymptomatic partners in the conjoint treatment of sexual dysfunction. *Journal of Sex and Marital Therapy,* 1979, 5(2), 79-89.

Cole, C., Chan, F., Blakeney, P., & Chesney, A. Participants' reactions to components of a rapid-treatment workshop for sexual dysfunction. *Journal of Sex and Marital Therapy,* 1980, *6*(1), 30-39.

Crooks, R., & Baur, K. *Our sexuality.* Menlo Park, Calif.: Benjamin-Cummings, 1980.

Frank, E., Anderson, C., & Rubinstein, D. Frequency of sexual dysfunction in "normal" couples. *The New England Journal of Medicine,* 1978, *299*(3), 111-115.

Lief, H. Marital and sex therapy must be integrated. *Sexuality Today Newsletter* 1982, *5*(40), 3. 3.

Masters, W., & Johnson, V. *Human sexual inadequacy.* Boston: Little, Brown, 1970.

Masters, W., Johnson, V., & Kolodny, R. *Human sexuality.* Boston: Little, Brown, 1982.

Powell, L., Blakeney, P., & Croft, H. Rapid treatment approach to human sexual inadequacy. *American Journal of Obstetrics and Gynecology,* 1974, *119,* 89-97.

Witkin, M. Sex therapy as an aid to marital and family therapy. *Journal of Sex and Marital Therapy,* 1977, *3*(1), 19-30.

4. Sexuality in Divorce and Remarriage

Jane Divita Woody, PhD, MSW
Associate Professor
School of Social Work
University of Nebraska at Omaha
Omaha, Nebraska

GARY, A 30-YEAR-OLD MAN DIVORCED FOR FOUR YEARS, CAME FOR therapy regarding erectile dysfunction with his current partner, Patricia, who was in the process of divorce and had two young children. Because Patricia had been diagnosed as alcohol dependent and had been in treatment, her husband had temporary custody of the children pending a final hearing. He had sought the divorce after learning of his wife's relationship with Gary and after a few sessions of marriage counseling.

Gary had many doubts about the relationship. He was aware that he might be an alternate form of dependency for Patricia. At the same time, he realized that he too may have been having a dependency relationship with her. Recently, he had become more interested in a committed relationship, tiring of the casual sexual encounters he had sought in the first few years after his divorce. Patricia seemed to fit his ideal of the kind of woman he could marry; however, she was a more reserved sexual partner than he would have liked. Patricia was reluctant to enter any therapy designed to explore Gary's sexual dysfunction or the possible differences in their sexual attitudes.

This case synopsis captures well the complexities involved in the therapeutic task of assessing the influence of various factors—individual, relationship, crisis—that contribute to a client's sexual problem. The particular crisis of concern here is divorce.

Divorce and its aftermath will very likely have some degree of impact on the individual's sexual self-concept. However, the nature and degree of that impact will vary widely, depending on the unique experience of each person. Just as the status of being married does not necessarily provide a healthy sexual self-concept or ensure adequate sexual functioning, so too the divorce process does not necessarily lead to a significant sexual identity crisis. Typically, though, divorce requires that certain adjustments related to sexuality be made. The family therapist should be familiar with the dynamics of at least the most common sex-related problems faced by clients during the divorce adjustment or remarriage processes. This article will focus on three specific areas: the impact of divorce on the sexual self-concept, the affair as a factor in divorce, and sexuality in remarriage. The goal is to provide therapists with a basis for assessing the unique influences of divorce and remarriage and to examine appropriate techniques that can be incorporated into the total treatment approach.

THE IMPACT OF DIVORCE ON THE SEXUAL SELF-CONCEPT

As a crisis event, divorce results in several different kinds of losses, which exert a powerful influence on the self-concept, the sexual self, and intimacy needs. The stages of emotional divorce described in the literature show that there is a normative process typical of persons who divorce. Given these stages and clinical experience, one can extrapolate to describe expectable assaults on the sexual self-concept.

Kessler (1975) identifies seven stages of emotional divorce: disillusionment, erosion, detachment, physical separation, mourning, exploration and hard work, and emotional freedom.

Disillusionment

The disillusionment stage can be a healthy steppingstone toward strengthening a marriage if the couple comes to see and accept each other realistically instead of insisting on totally egocentric or idealistic expectations. If, however, a couple fails to accept and negotiate or modify their differences, they typically move on to the stage of erosion, which takes its toll through a variety of means—destructive verbal and nonverbal communication, lack of support and attention, and avoidance and isolation.

Erosion and Detachment

In the next stages the overall relationship is attacked; however, only the sexual relationship will be dealt with here. The exact form of the attack will vary, depending on many factors, for example, the quality of the sex relationship, communication about sex, the overall relationship, individual personality characteristics, the stage each partner is in, etc. Because of the diversity of factors involved, patterns for coping with erosion and detachment are innumerable; a few of the most common are described.

"Let's Make Up" is a pattern wherein one or both partners may sincerely want to improve the overall relationship. This is demonstrated through a period of increased affection and sexual responsiveness. If this effort fails, feelings of disappointment and sexual inadequacy or unattractiveness often result. "Prove Your Love" is a pattern in which one partner copes by selfishly increasing sexual demands, with the result that sex either becomes a battleground or the other partner gives in to sex with anger and resentment and becomes passive and unresponsive. Under such circumstances, the sex act and the whole area of sexuality become associated with negative feelings. "Any Port in a Storm" characterizes the pattern in which one or both partners avoid all intimacy, affection, and sex until such time as one or both have an extreme physical need for sexual release. The result is either guilt at having used the partner or rage and resentment at having been used. Such feelings can lead to further reactions, ranging from increased aloofness and estrangement to verbal and physical abuse.

These few patterns are presented to emphasize the point that, before physical separation, couples will probably have gone through a variety of coping maneuvers, all with impact on their sexuality. The sexual self-concept is apt to be in an extremely vulnerable, if not a bruised and battered, state. During the stages of erosion and detachment, the person often seeks solace and personal validation through casual sexual contacts or an affair; obviously, these new situations have even further effect on the couple's sexual relationship and on each individual's sexual adjustment. The affair as a factor in divorce will be dealt with separately in a later section.

Physical Separation and Mourning

Feelings of abandonment, betrayal, loneliness, continued attachment to the partner, and desperation at feeling unloved and possibly unlovable are typical of the separation and mourning stages. The intensity with which a person experiences these feelings may depend on whether he or she was the initiator or the deserted, or whether the decision was truly a joint one with both partners equal in their emotional divorce from each other. The sense of being either in or out of control with regard to the decision is crucial, since having made the choice and being in control can give strong rational footing when one is about to sink into the inevitable emotional morass that accompanies these stages.

Weiss (1975) has noted how separated and divorced partners continue to feel drawn toward the partner, pine for him or her, and attempt to relieve anxiety by contact of some kind. These feelings may not be strictly sexual, but they are part and parcel of the person's sexuality. The need may be for intimacy that includes giving and receiving affection and comfort and generally sharing oneself. Or the person may experience strong sexual desire and associate that with previous sexual experiences with the former partner and long for fulfillment.

Ways of coping with all of these ambivalent feelings are innumerable. It is not uncommon for partners in the early stages of separation and divorce to have sporadic or even regular sexual contacts with each other. Others cope by engaging in casual or promiscuous sexual encounters. Some move quickly to establish a new committed intimate relationship. At the other end of the continuum, some persons lose awareness of themselves as sexual beings and of their sexual needs and avoid all sexual activity, including masturbation.

Exploration, Hard Work, and Emotional Freedom

The work of self-exploration and self-understanding following divorce is painful. Since there are many other demands and stresses placed on divorced persons, it is no wonder that many simply bypass these goals. They may get stuck in the mourning stage, unable to move beyond the anger and sadness that are normal when a relationship has been lost. As these normal feelings hang on, they may turn into maladaptive rage and depression and form the basis for continued hostility with the ex-spouse and dysfunctional parent-child relationships. Others may form a premature attachment or dependency on a new partner as a way of coping with feelings of inadequacy or fear of starting over as an independent person. Yet it is only through self-exploration and self-understanding that the person can clarify his or her own contribution to the demise of the marriage, gain awareness of individual needs and goals, explore the various ways to fulfill these in the future, and learn how to assume responsiblity for one's own happiness.

The following case illustrates a common pattern of how couples move toward emotional divorce at different paces, each coping independently and usually ineffectively with the pain of alienation, and finally using the legal system to cope with the vestiges of ambivalent feelings toward the spouse.

Sherry had felt early in their four years of marriage that communication between her and Bud was poor. Bud never mentioned much about his job as a small-town policeman (though he freely recounted incidents about the job to his parents). Sherry resented his unilateral decision to build a house for them over her objections that it would strap them financially. He alone decided on the design of the house and began to spend all of his spare time doing the construction himself. After their baby was born, Sherry felt even more strongly that Bud saw her only as wife and mother and himself as family provider. She tried to talk to him about her needs, but apparently Bud was so wrapped up in his job, building the house, and financial worries that he could not really hear her message. She began to detach herself from the situation. She continued to have sex with Bud, but it was strictly for him; she felt he did not even notice her lack of involvement, nor did he seem to care about her needs for affection or sexual satisfaction. As a result, her silent detachment and resentment grew.

When Sherry took a job to help out with the finances, she found an outlet in her co-workers (mostly men) for her unfulfilled needs to be a person, to share herself with others, and to communicate more openly. As she gained a stronger sense of her own identity and goals in life, she decided she could not find fulfillment in the marriage and filed for divorce. Her decision came as a complete shock to Bud. While he acknowledged that her account of their relationship was accurate, he felt he had really heard her message and wanted a chance for them to work on the marriage. Sherry, however, had already emotionally divorced herself from the relationship.

Bud, as the deserted partner, was in an extremely vulnerable state. He felt he had been a failure as a husband and as a sexual partner. When he guessed that Sherry had had a sexual relationship with one of her co-workers, he was filled with anger and a sense of betrayal that was especially painful as he recalled that he would never have considered being unfaithful, though he had had plenty of opportunities. Bud vacillated between these feelings and a sense of despair that there was no second chance for him. He felt totally out of control and consciously acknowledged that the only thing he could have any say about was the custody of their 2-year-old daughter. Consequently, he invested his energy in fighting Sherry for custody and won. After his victory, he had no interest in sex and could not imagine himself ever getting involved with another woman. When he left counseling, a major risk to him and his child was that he would overinvest himself in the father role and create an unhealthy symbiotic relationship with his young daughter.

Sherry, too, was in a vulnerable state. For her, it remained questionable whether her decision to divorce Bud was based on a strong sense of her own identity or whether it was based on the security gained from the relationship she had had with her co-worker. From time to time, Bud's sexual slurs and name calling came back to haunt her, and she had to acknowledge the fact that her infidelity had cost her custody of her child. These were the threads with which Sherry had to work in reweaving the fabric of her sexual identity and future sexual adjustment.

Implications for Therapy

During the stages of divorce adjustment there are several common problems relevant to sexuality that clients often present. Although the problem may not appear overtly sexual, the task of the therapist is to be tuned into the sexual implications, understand the sexual dynamics, and be comfortable enough and competent enough to give the client permission to deal with it and instill confidence that it can be solved.

Loneliness is one of the most painful feelings that accompany divorce. The individual often experiences hopelessness at facing the prospect of making new friends as a single person. Clients complain that they do not know where or how to meet people. The loneliness can turn to depression when they have tried singles' bars or experienced the frantic search to pair up that is common in certain self-help divorce adjustment groups. The therapist must help the person (1) get in touch with his or her own motives and needs, (2) explore the extent to which sexual needs are part of the loneliness, (3) understand the extent to which fantasy of a new ideal partner or of the ex-spouse dominates their efforts to make new friends, and (4) evaluate options for dealing with the problem in terms of where the person is in the divorce adjustment process.

Anxiety about newly achieved sexual freedom and the changes that have taken place in sexual codes and behaviors is another common problem. Some persons appear to enjoy the freedom to have many new sexual partners without commitment; others find oppressive the expectation that they must have sex with every new friend or date. Somewhere between these two extremes, others explore by trial and error their new sexual self-concept. As clients cope with the dating and sex game, they often find they have to confront additional feelings of anger at having been used sexually, guilt over sexually exploiting others, or depression when intimacy needs are not met. In addition, both male and female clients often express concerns about the new emphasis on the female orgasm and other changes in sexual mores. For these kinds of sex-related anxieties, the therapist must help the client (1) recognize specific fears and anxieties, (2) bring to consciousness personal needs, expectations, and values about sexuality, and (3) hasten the reintegration of the sexual self so that the person can deal openly and honestly with potential sexual partners and choose whether to engage in sex and on what terms. It is only with this kind of self-knowledge and comfort with one's own needs and values that a person can communicate honestly about sex and take responsibility for his or her own sexuality, thus gaining protection from the hazards of trial-and-error sexual encounters.

Specific sexual dysfunctions may appear during the divorce process. Loss of sexual desire, erectile dysfunction, premature ejaculation, and orgasmic difficulties may be present either alone or in the context of the kinds of problems discussed above. The therapeutic assessment must encompass the individual's previous sexual functioning, the dynamics of the previous marriage, the overall impact of the divorce process on the person's sexual self-concept, and the present circumstances in which the sex dysfunction is manifested. Regarding the extent to which the problem existed in the previous marriage and the possibility that it may have been a factor in the divorce, the therapist will have to be content with the client's version of the problem and its causes. The direction that the therapy takes will obviously depend on the overall assessment and on the therapist's level of competence for treating sex dysfunctions.

THE AFFAIR AS A FACTOR IN DIVORCE

When an affair, on the part of either one or both partners, has been a factor in the decision to divorce, the tasks of postdivorce adjustment are further complicated. Without resolution of the infidelity and its sequelae, the result may be an embittered or chaotic relationship between the ex-spouses that can delay or totally prevent a healthy reintegration of the self-concept.

Recent research has found a slight increase in extramarital sex among males but a marked increase for females; predictions are that the greater freedom of sexual expression for both men and women will bring increasing risks to the permanence of marriage and higher divorce rates (Kessler, 1975). It is therefore critical for therapists to understand the additional assaults on the identity and the sexual self-concept that may occur when infidelity has been a factor in divorce.

The affair, regardless of all of its other possible facets, has a powerful sexual component, and it is often this that causes people the most grief and has the most impact on their future sexual adjustment. There are a number of variables to consider: the affair may be an insignificant diversion, an important substitute for an already dead marital relationship, or something in between; discovery of the affair may or may not lead to immediate breakup of the marriage or of the extramarital relationship; a couple may try to work through the trauma either with or without professional help or choose to bypass understanding and "start over" as if the affair never happened.

Only a few aspects of infidelity, the ensuing feelings, and sex-related adjustment problems can be covered here, but the issues and therapeutic implications discussed have application to a broad range of concerns.

It is typical to think of the "wronged" partner as having the most serious or painful problems, and it may very well be that the worst effects do accrue to this person. It may take greater therapeutic skill and empathy to help the client who is in or has had the affair. The person may be struggling with the need to understand motivations that led to the relationship, guilt about the pain brought to the marital or extramarital partner, conflicts about whether the affair was worth the price of loss of the marriage and loss of one's "real family," self-recriminations at one's own stupidity in handling the affair or not realizing the risks, and, finally, possible doubts about the strength of the extramarital relationship and the wisdom of either ending it or making a commitment to it.

This latter concern centers on the viability of the affair relationship. Questions about the new liaison may surface at the point of divorce, when the remarriage takes place, or when the remarriage relationship is in trouble. Following the decision to divorce, individuals involved in an affair can usually benefit from counseling, especially if they plan to marry the affair partner soon. However, it is fairly common for such clients to resist analysis of the relationship; they may not wish to confront issues of dependency, the need for individuation, and the implications for the custody decision and their future relationship with their children. For example, when Marie and Ted (both 40) came for marriage counseling, Marie had already decided on divorce. She had recently become involved with a classmate she had met again at a high school reunion. She had left Ted and gone to another state to spend several weekends with this man, who was divorced and had custody of his four children. She intended to move in with him as soon as her divorce was final and was willing to give up custody of her teen-age son. Since the marriage had been a happy and successful one, except for a very brief relationship Ted had had seven years before, mention was made of options such as separation, or even living on her own before making a new love commitment. Marie would consider no other options and no further counseling.

As for the wronged partner, the most significant cause of pain may be the sense of having had no control over the situation, whereas the other partner appeared to be in control. Related to this is the confusing and painful feeling of having been betrayed. American marriages are still based on the expectation of fidelity, and this apparently holds true regardless of dissatisfaction with a marriage, the insignificance of the affair, or current ideas about freedom of sexual expression (Pietropinto & Simenauer, 1977).

After the immediate reactions of shock and disbelief have passed, it appears that common mechanisms for coping with the sense of betrayal are self-recriminations at having trusted the partner, anger at oneself for having remained faithful, and fantasies of being unfaithful (and sometimes carrying out the fantasy). The person may imagine a romantic or sexual relationship in which he or she once again feels valued, loved, and desired by a partner; the fantasy may also include letting the partner discover the affair and relishing the revenge.

Another constellation of feelings centers on preoccupation with the details of the spouse's affair. Wanting to know the logistics, the reasons, the specifics of the affection, communication, sex acts, etc., represents an attempt on the part of the wronged partner to gain a sense of control of the situation through access to information that only the other partner has.

Because of the strong sexual focus of an affair, the wronged partner often readily assumes the cloak of sexual inadequacy or unattractiveness and sees these as the cause. He or she dwells on previous sexual behaviors or encounters suggestive of possible shortcomings, magnifies these, and blames them for the infidelity. Comparisons with the affair partner may become an obsession, for example, "He never did like my small breasts" or "I should have kissed and held her more like she asked me to."

These kinds of feelings are strongest upon initial discovery of the affair, but they often remain with the wronged partner long after the divorce. Flashbacks of the discovery of infidelity, of attempts to confront the partner, or of the ways the couple discussed and dealt with it are commonly experienced from time to time. Since these are often triggered by a myriad of stimuli over which the person has little control, feelings of being out of control may once again flood the psyche. A final and more persistent effect may be seen in the person's attitude toward future intimate relationships. At one extreme is the neurotic seeking of self-validation and sexual adequacy through promiscuous or casual risk-taking sexual encounters, and at the other extreme is the loss of trust in the possibility of a new meaningful relationship.

Understanding the history of the couple from the time of discovery to the divorce may be critical in helping the client. Between these times, the couple may have separated, reconciled, continued to have sex, or tried to reinvest in the relationship, and they may have engaged in these behaviors several times over. Moreover, all of these behaviors carry the potential of either healing or further damaging each partner's self-esteem and sexual self-concept. For example, if there was a period of ambivalence in which the spouse would neither give up the affair nor give up the marriage, the final results could vary. Jeannie was a client who had counseling during her husband's ambivalent period; she hung on to the hope of trying to win his commitment to her and the family; but when six months passed without resolution she became severely depressed and was too incapacitated to take action. A different situation, however, occurred with John, a client whose case is presented in further detail below. Although his wife, Louise, had ended her affair, she remained totally detached and could not reinvest in the marriage. When John could no longer cope with the constant state of disequilibrium that brought on high blood pressure, insomnia, and a prostate infection, he found the strength to emotionally detach himself from Louise and make the decision to divorce.

John (31) and Louise (29) had been married for 10 years and had a 6-year-old daughter. They had a history of sexual incompatibility, with Louise having little interest in sex. John, who acknowledged that from their first meeting even through the divorce he was completely in love with his wife, had through the years adjusted to her preferences by showing consideration of her feelings and by making few sexual demands.

Since John's job required him to travel a great deal, Louise gradually became emotionally detached from him, generally feeling more comfortable when he was gone. John regularly called home and talked to her; he reported that although he was very lonely away from home, he had never even considered having a sexual relationship with any woman other than Louise. When they were together on weekends, there was little communication, other than updating each other on the family business, for which Louise was primarily responsible in John's absence.

Louise entered a brief affair with an older man with whom she had to deal in business. She did not initiate the intimacy but invested herself tremendously in this man. She "fell in love" with him, engaged in sex, and hoped to get pregnant; she never considered the possible complications that her behavior might have for her marriage and family. She was shocked at her partner's lack of reciprocal feeling for her and at his insensitivity to her wish to get pregnant. She broke off the relationship because of what she considered his cavalier attitude, but remained in love with him.

Following John's discovery of the affair, John and Louise received marriage counseling, including both joint and individual sessions. Louise felt she could not reinvest in the marriage and neither partner was ready to end the marriage. They chose, for over a year, to remain stalemated, seeking counseling sessions intermittently as their stress became unmanageable. John eventually arrived at the understanding that there was no basis for a marriage and that his continued acceptance of the status quo was highly self-destructive. When he made the decision to divorce, Louise offered no resistance and immediately began moving toward her independent goals.

Implications for Therapy

The therapeutic tasks in divorce adjustment counseling are indeed complicated by an extramarital affair. The most basic issue is for therapists to be aware of their own feelings and experiences regarding infidelity and assess the extent to which they can be helpful when this highly emotional factor is involved. It is critical to be able to deal with the client's pain, let the person explore and "own" it, and subsequently to help him or her make some sense of it. L'Abate and L'Abate (1979) have offered a framework for this task in explaining intimate relationships as inherently rendering the partners vulnerable to hurt from each other. Gaining this kind of intellectual understanding can be an important first step in the client's attempt to make sense of the extreme pain associated with infidelity.

The client can also benefit from a post-mortem analysis of the past relationship. Insight into the dynamics of the marital relationship, of the needs of both partners and of the extent to which these needs did or did not mesh may increase rational understanding of why the affair happened. It is important to help the client explore his or her contribution to the failure of the marriage and also to realistically assess whether the affair was an effective or ineffective way for the partner to have coped. The ultimate goal of increasing rational understanding is to help the client accept the reality that the affair, the divorce, and the pain are all a part of the person's new history and that they were due to many reasons—not simply to the client's personal inadequacy. From that point, the therapist can assist the person to move on to the goal of reintegration of the self and progress toward emotional freedom.

SEXUALITY IN REMARRIAGE

Remarriage definitely has significant implications for the sexuality of all family members—adults and children. Very similar dynamics also apply to the "living together" arrangement, which has become an increasingly common pattern for divorced persons (as well as for never-married singles). The sexual issues involved in these family structures need to be acknowledged and confronted.

Following divorce, both parents and children necessarily expend a great deal of physical and psychic energy in adjusting to the changes. The complicated tasks for adults have been outlined in the discussions above. As for children, not only must they continue with their age-related tasks of development, but they must also cope with the many losses and changes associated with divorce—loss of the previous intact family and the parental pair; new modes of relating to both parents; the feelings brought on by the divorce; and oftentimes, new living arrangements and routines, including, perhaps, a new community, neighborhood, house, and school.

Attempting to balance and meet the needs of parents and children during this period becomes even more difficult when a parent, or both parents, begin to date, become involved in a serious, committed relationship, or remarry. The situation is likely to be even harder to deal with if it happens soon after the divorce. The parent entering the new relationship should assume the most responsibility for being sensitive to the children's needs under these circumstances. However, the ex-spouse, in his or her co-parenting role, also has a responsibility for the children's welfare. The extent to which both parents can deal with this development of new relationships will depend on how much progress they themselves have made through the stages of divorce adjustment. They will be most capable if they have done the hard work of self-exploration, gained understanding and acceptance of the divorce, arrived at a strong sense of their own individual identities, and ended the spousal relationship and developed a cooperative co-parenting relationship. However, this ideal is probably the exception rather than the rule. Therefore, therapists often find the opportunity to counsel clients who are experiencing family problems with respect to dating, living with someone, or remarriage; it is not unusual for the problems to be rooted in the unfinished business of adjustment to the divorce.

By necessity, this discussion can focus on only a few critical problem areas associated with remarriage and sexuality. The first area deals with balancing the adult's intimacy and sexual needs with the children's needs, in conjunction with their level of cognitive and emotional development and their degree of adjustment to the divorce. The second area deals with sexual assumptions and codes within the remarriage family.

The Love Needs of Both Adults and Children

Emotions for both parents and children usually begin to work overtime as one or both parents begin to date. Doubts abound as to how to explain this behavior to the children and whether it will confuse or harm them. In addition, unresolved feelings about the ex-spouse can lead to further concerns about the ex-spouse's opinion and what he or she will say to the children about the dating and vice versa. Clients raise such questions as "How much should I explain about my needs to my child?" "Should I have my date meet the children?" "Should we do things together with the children?" "Should we spend the night or weekend together with the children present?" "My children react so differently to my dates . . . the 6-year-old is always friendly, but the 10-year-old is surly and won't speak. Why is that?" Similar questions emerge as the parent moves toward a more serious relationship or toward marriage.

At some point most divorced adults realize that they must look after their own needs for companionship, sexual intimacy, and individuation, this latter including other identity components beyond the parenting role. The parent, however, must feel secure in the fact that meeting these needs represents no disloyalty to the children or former spouse. Having dates, exploring new relationships, and even engaging in casual sexual encounters (with clear understanding of the terms) can be beneficial to self-esteem and to reintegration of the person's identity. Regarding casual sex, the person may consciously choose not to rush prematurely into a deep or committed relationship. If, however, sex with a partner is still desired, clear and honest communication about the meaning of the sex is necessary so that neither person is deceived or exploited. The newly single person may wisely use a range of interpersonal experiences as an opportunity to gain increased understanding and acceptance of his or her sexuality and sexual needs, which could form the basis for a healthier sexual adjustment than was obtained in the previous marriage relationship.

Children likewise have love needs and other needs that will affect their ability to adjust to their parents' single status and all that it implies. Children need the security of feeling loved by both parents and knowing that they are not going to lose that love relationship with either parent as a result of a parent's dating or committed relationship or remarriage. Gaining this security comes in time with the opportunity to adapt to both parents as single persons and to two separate parent-child relationships. Since divorce alone brings on many changes, when a parent's new love relationship follows closely and brings even more life changes, stress levels may become almost unmanageable.

Balancing both parental and child love needs is indeed a tremendous challenge. The task may be easier if the parent (1) accepts the fact that stabilizing this new relationship within the family represents a process that will take time and trial-and-error learning, (2) seeks and accepts tentative answers for coping, and (3) remains sensitive to reactions and changes within the children and deals with these.

There are numerous pitfalls in this process. In the early stages of dating, problems may emerge if the parent seeks premature approval of the children for the dating partner or requires the children's involvement in family activities with that person. In addition, parents must expect children to react differently according to their own adjustment and age-related developmental tasks; for example, the adolescent's own emerging sexuality may trigger added conflicts about confronting the parent's intimacy and sexual needs. As a parent's love relationship becomes more serious, a child may feel even more threatened with losing the love of that parent or with having the new partner replace the other blood parent. When remarriage takes place, the couple faces the continuing task of consolidating themselves into a viable marital unit that assures the new partner an appropriate role within the family hierarchy. The remarriage family must accept the reality that it cannot be an instant family, that blending is an inherently disorganizing experience, and that issues regarding roles, rules, and routines will have to be consciously worked out (Goldner, 1982).

Working out issues related to love, affection, and sexuality can be particularly difficult. These tend to be taboo topics generally and may be avoided even more in the remarriage family. Instead of dealing with the issue directly and working it out according to the unique family situation, adults may assume that affection and other sexual issues between them or displays of affection toward the children will be handled as they were in the previous nuclear or single-parent family. Remarriage partners may not be any more comfortable in communicating openly about sex than they were in the previous marriage. Yet there are numerous sex-related issues that require open, conscious discussion and evaluation of options and outcomes (for example, whether to have a mutual child; the type of affection, bonding, and child care expected to occur between the stepparent and stepchildren; and the kind of affectionate exchanges between parents that will take place in front of children).

Children also need encouragement to express openly their concerns about love, affection, jealousies, etc., within the family. Often children's fears of loss of parental love or loss of their usual status in the family are manifested indirectly in hostilities to family members, requests to change custody, behavior problems in school and elsewhere, and premature disengagement from the family.

The intimate and sexual relationship of the remarried partners may become a barometer of their own and the children's total adjustment to the newly blended family. Extreme stress due to changes brought on by the new family structure may lead partners to depression and withdrawal from each other, to loss of sexual desire, or even to sexual dysfunction. Such ineffective coping mechanisms further cut off the opportunity for the couple to reenergize each other, strengthen the marital unit, and creatively deal with problems. A starting point for interrupting this destructive pattern would be for the couple to feel comfortable enough to openly discuss the most obvious symptom—the loss of affectional and sexual intimacy. In so doing, they may discover the underlying problem to be mother's anxiety about stepfather's disciplining of her children, or his feeling of being an intruder in the mother-children relationship, etc.

Sexual Assumptions and Codes within the Remarriage Family

The blending of two families to a large extent involves a transformation of the intimate world of all the individuals. The rituals of private life are suddenly upset, and the challenge is to arrive at a new, more comprehensive set of rules to organize intimate family behavior. A few of the more relevant issues include privacy, space allocation and usage, and affectional, sexual, and dress codes. For each individual, most of these issues have already been worked out satisfactorily in the previous family, largely as an unconscious process, so it is not surprising that family members might deny the reality that it has to be done over again and done as a conscious, open process (Goldner, 1982).

Consider but a few questions. Who gets the bathroom first? Who can help the younger children with their baths? Can anyone use the parents' shower? Where can the noisy blow dryer be used? Who can walk around in underclothes, nightgowns, or less? How long can one person stay in the bathroom? Who can lock doors? Who needs to knock on doors? Who can touch, hug, or kiss whom? Who can use profanity? Who can use nicknames or pet names? The list could go on and on. Knowing the right answers has critical importance for the overall comfort level of family members.

It may be most useful to explore one of these issues in depth, for example, the sexual taboo of incest.

This is a significant topic since more and more children are finding themselves in cohabiting arrangements or in stepfamily situations. Under these circumstances, where the incest taboo is not strong, the danger to children is magnified. Kessler (1975) has commented that confusion results as to who is or is not seducible in the household. Finkelhor's (1979) study reported the rate of father-daughter incest in families with stepfathers to be almost five times higher than in any other subgroups in his survey. In addition, girls with stepfathers were found to be more vulnerable to sexual victimization by other men outside the family as well. Finkelhor speculates that this vulnerability may be due to various causes: greater family disorganization, less parental supervision, permeable family boundaries permitting male friends and relatives into the home who are less protective of daughters, and serious emotional conflicts within the daughter related to feelings of loss of the mother's love and the need to compete with her for attention from men. Unfortunately, the potential for sexual victimization is typically not faced until violations have occurred.

As uncomfortable as it may be, family members need to deal openly with each other regarding space, privacy, and affection. Expectations must be clearly delineated and family rules negotiated and enforced. The family must find ways to meet needs of members so as to promote the healthy development of all. For example, partners must clearly express the fact that their expectation of sexual fidelity means that children and stepchildren are not to be treated as potential sex objects or partners. They cannot assume that each knows what kind of dress, conversation topics, and displays of affection to the children are appropriate and acceptable to the spouse. Neither should the parents assume that the children will automatically know what are the appropriate kinds of interaction with the adults or other children in the household.

On the surface, the risk of violations of the incest taboo seems greatest if there are adolescent children in the family; however, this may not always be the case. First, since the young person's sexual qualities are obvious, the adults may be more likely to confront the sexual implications of family rituals and behaviors than with younger children. Second, teen-agers themselves, because of their normal thrust toward independence, their verbal abilities, and their tendency to question adult authority, may be more likely than a young child to state preferences or report dissatisfaction with a situation. The family with young children may be more likely to harbor the unconscious fantasy to be like the previous blood family and let things take their "normal" course.

> The Rogers family consisted of Tom (30), not previously married, Jean (33), their 4-month-old mutual baby daughter, and Jean's son Randy (9) and daughter Susie (6), both children of her former marriage to Bob Smith. Bob and his new wife, Jenny, not previously married, live in the same town as the Rogers, have no children of their own, and have regular visitation with Randy and Susie every other weekend.
>
> Jean and Bob were divorced when Susie was 4, and both remarried within the year. Misunderstandings, conflicts, and hostilities have con-

tinued between the two families in the two years since the divorce. The Smiths brought a complaint against the Rogers after Susie told her father and stepmother that Tom, her mother's new husband, was touching her in a way she did not like. Susie reported that Tom often bathed her and rubbed her buttocks and touched the vaginal area; she said he also did this when he put her to bed at night, often tickling her and rubbing her under her pajamas and underpants. Sometimes this happened when she was sitting on his lap. The child also said that she did not like Tom calling her "Sexy Susie."

Without attempting to untangle the dynamics of this situation, at least several key factors should be mentioned. Both remarriages closely following the divorce required a mammoth adjustment effort of both sets of adults and the children. In addition, Tom and Jean's new baby daughter added stresses to their relationship and to Randy and Susie's sense of belonging to the remarriage family. As Jean focused more on caring for the baby and Tom took over some of her usual responsibilities for nurturing Susie, it appears that Susie accepted this change on the surface. A 6-year-old child has strong needs for affection and attention from parents and these were likely intensified with the arrival of the new baby, who received much of the mother's attention. Neither Tom nor Jean appeared to be aware that Tom had violated Susie's sense of privacy and body boundaries. Neither had openly dealt with the strains in their intimate relationship, the extent to which their individual needs were being met, their expectations regarding expression of affection toward Jean's children, or the appropriateness of the sexualized atmosphere set by the couple's own behavior in front of the chldren.

Implications for Therapy

Problems relevant to the intimate routines of family life may be manifested directly or indirectly; they may appear early in the formation of the family or years later; and their vestiges may continue to plague individual family members long after they have left the remarriage family experience.

It is important for therapists to be familiar with a few guidelines unique to working with remarriage families so that these can be appropriately integrated with other treatment approaches.

Perhaps the most basic issue relates to the therapist's beliefs about the "family." The remarriage family is best understood as a new and different family form, not a simple variation of the nuclear family. This concept needs to be conveyed to family members, who may resist it in favor of retaining an image of the "real family" from the past. A second task is to help the family become willing to observe itself and its processes and to accept the necessity for openly dealing with any issue and resolving it with negotiated rules that are congruent as much as possible with the needs of all members. These two attitudes are critical if the family is to work together, allowing themselves time for the complex process of building a new family. A final therapeutic guideline is to help members openly verbalize their comfort level with the intimate rituals of family life. These often involve sexual issues and unconscious needs and feelings that clients all too readily bypass. The therapist must have the skill to give clients permission to deal with such topics, either by directly or routinely raising them as a part of the interview or by exploration of indirect cues or direct comments.

CONCLUSION

In becoming aware of the complex tasks facing divorced and remarriage families, therapists should carefully assess their practice of marriage and family therapy and move toward integrating prevention efforts into their usual treatment formats (Woody, 1978). The potential for sex-related problems is present, although clients may not bring these as primary complaints. Prevention efforts require an open, directive approach to sexual matters and a strong educational thrust in letting clients know what to expect from the divorce and remarriage processes.

There are usually various opportunities for these activities. In marriage counseling, when divorce looms large as an option, the therapist should encourage clients to do extensive reality testing regarding their images of themselves as divorced individuals and single parents, what they expect their intimacy and social needs to be, and how they see themselves pursuing these. In actual divorce adjustment counseling, exploration of intimacy and sexual needs should be a routine part of therapy so as to give clients early permission to deal with these important areas (Woody, 1981).

Any strong preventive effort regarding possible hazards for remarriage families requires the therapist to be sensitive to the fact that remarriage is conceivable for the client at any stage of the divorce adjustment process; consequently, this potential could also be routinely explored so as to provide at least a beginning opportunity to confront the complexities involved in remarriage. Finally, in actual counseling with remarriage families, the therapist must again be willing to provide education and be able to encourage the family to deal with the intimate and sexual facets of life that are inevitably involved in the task of building a new family.

REFERENCES

Finkelhor, D. *Sexually victimized children*. New York: Free Press, 1979.

Goldner, V. Remarriage family: Structure, system, future. In L. Messinger (Ed.), *Therapy with remarriage families*. Rockville, Md.: Aspen Systems Corp., 1982.

Kessler, S. *The American way of divorce: Prescriptions for change*. Chicago: Nelson-Hall, 1975.

L'Abate, L., & L'Abate, B. The paradoxes of intimacy. *Family Therapy*, 1979, 6, 175-184.

Pietropinto, A., & Simenauer, J. *Beyond the male myth*. New York: Quadrangle/New York Times Book Co., 1977.

Weiss, R.S. *Marital separation*. New York: Basic Books, 1975.

Woody, J. Preventive interventions for children of divorce. *Social Casework*, 1978, 59, 537-544.

Woody, J. Transition from marital therapy to divorce adjustment therapy. In A.S. Gurman (Ed.), *Questions and answers in the practice of family therapy*. New York: Brunner/Mazel, 1981.

5. Homosexual and Bisexual Issues

Leslie E. Collins, PhD, MSW
Assistant Professor
Psychiatry and Behavioral Sciences
School of Medicine
Creighton University
Omaha, Nebraska

Nathalia Zimmerman, ACSW
Assistant Professor
Psychiatry and Behavioral Sciences
School of Medicine
Creighton University
Omaha, Nebraska

W HEN THE "OTHER WOMAN" OR THE "OTHER MAN" TURNS OUT TO BE of the same gender as the client, the family therapist is faced with an unexpected challenge. Too often, the note of courage that precedes such a disclosure gets lost in the silence of the therapist's discomfort and uncertainty, or subtle rejection. Similar pitfalls and opportunities prevail when the therapist is faced with a family convulsed with the discovery or declaration of a gay, lesbian, or bisexual orientation by one of its children. This article presents one perspective on family therapy with mixed-orientation couples and families with a bisexual or homosexual child. It is offered as an approach toward more adequately meeting the challenges and opportunities that such families provide.

MIXED-ORIENTATION COUPLES

With the application of social science research methodologies to the study of bisexuality and homosexuality, it has become increasingly clear that unilinear explanations and dichotomous classifications miss much of the complexity and range of human sexuality. Research utilizing extensive nonanecdotal data has cast serious and pervasive doubt upon traditional psychoanalytic theories of bisexuality and homosexuality. There has been, as documented by Bayer (1981), a widespread challenge of those professional orthodoxies that sometimes have served to exacerbate suffering rather than to alleviate it. In one of the relatively few national samples of gay men and lesbian women, Robinson, Skeen, Hobson, and Herrman (1982) examined the parent-child relationships of their respondents. Out of their sample of 322, two-thirds saw their relationships with their fathers as "extremely satisfactory" or "satisfactory," while over three-fourths perceived their relationships with their mothers as "extremely satisfactory" or "satisfactory." Such research does not agree with traditional psychoanalytic theory. On the other hand, of course, it does not deny the relevance of traditional explanations of homosexual behavior in specific cases. In general, however, dysfunctional parental relationships appear to be neither necessary nor sufficient conditions for the appearance and existence of bisexuality or homosexuality, a view also supported by Hooker (1969), and Bell, Weinberg, and Hammersmith (1981).

While bisexuality and homosexuality per se can no longer be considered pathological in any objective, measurable sense, it is undeniable that a bisexual or homosexual person married to someone who is heterosexual may well find his or her orientation a source of concern and conflict, both for himself or herself as well as for the partner should this orientation be discovered or disclosed. Some spouses never discover their partner's orientation, others know but do not mention it, while a few interact with the bisexual and homosexual community with a knowledge of their partner's orientation and an apparent acceptance of a socially variant life style (Warren, 1976).

For any particular bisexual or homosexual person, the reasons for getting married are likely to represent some mixture of social and familial pressures to marry, a desire to cure one's orientation (Ross, 1972), the hope of escaping the social opprobrium attached to being homosexual, dissatisfaction with the local gay or lesbian "scene," desire for children, or self-deception and simple ignorance. Even following an awareness of their gay or lesbian feelings, most gay or lesbian spouses remain married for some time, feeling, in the words of Voeller and Walters (1978), "locked in" to the marriage and their responsibilities to their children, their spouses, or both.

There is little research on successful accommodation in mixed-orientation couples. In Ross's 1972 study of eleven Belgian mixed-orientation couples, all had considered separation or divorce initially, but had rejected it because of concerns for the children, enjoyment of a shared home life, companionship of a platonic nature, social respectability, and fear of inability to live an independent life. Voeller and Walters (1978) suggest that there are three styles of resolving the internal and external strains of a mixed-orientation relationship: divorce or separation; a friendly nonsexual accommodation within the relationship; or an open or semi-open relationship in which one or both of the partners is sexually active outside the relationship. Saghir and Robins (1973) found that 9% of the lesbians and 12% of the gays in their sample were married. None of the spouses, however, were aware of the homosexual involvement of their partners. The survival of a mixed-orientation marriage in which the bisexual or homosexual partner continued active relationships with the knowledge of the spouse was considered unlikely.

In Rifkin's study (1968), married bisexuals and homosexuals maintained relatively clear heterosexual interest. That is, heterosexual stimulation was an omnipresent factor, while homosexual activity tended to be episodic and an indicator of stress within the relationship. The most common factor relating to extended homosexual episodes in this sample was a situation that threatened the bisexual or homosexual partner's sense of adequacy, competency, or potency. Job and business crises were most often involved. Sporadic homosexual episodes were more often the outcome of problems in the home or with the family, with unresolved questions of control and dominancy being at issue.

It is doubtful that an accurate estimate exists of the percentage of supposedly heterosexual marriages that are in fact composed of mixed-orientation couples. What is clear is that the number of couple members who either
initiate therapy because of this aspect of their relationship or for whom it
becomes a central issue during the course of their therapy is apparently
increasing. If this impression is at all reality based, perhaps the increased
availability of sexual information, not to mention misinformation, and the
gradual improvement in the social acceptability of serious discussion of
human sexuality in part account for the growing availability of
mixed-orientation couples for therapy. Nor can the permission-giving
aspects of the human rights and gay rights movements be ignored.

A FAMILY THERAPY PERSPECTIVE

The clinician treating families where bisexuality or homosexuality is an
issue needs a treatment model that allows both for the validation and change
of the sexual orientation and behavior of each member, while offering a
conceptual framework to identify dysfunctional aspects presented as symptoms. It is crucial that the therapist *not* consider sexual orientation per se to
be "the problem." The model developed by Terkelson (1980), which links
therapeutic change to adult development and family life cycle, is eminently
suited to this task.

According to this model, the family is a social organization characterized
by permanency of membership and by the affectional relationships of its
members. Its purpose is to provide a context that supports need attainment
for its members. Ideally, the family structure, expressed in patterned sequences of behavior, evolves in order to satisfy those needs, while development of any individual member triggers change in family structure through a
process of need-signaling behavior. Destabilization of the family system
ensues, followed by a restabilization when the structure alters to meet and
integrate this developmental need. At the same time, deletion of old, less
functionally relevant behavior occurs.

The family system, in this situation, is faced with change as expressed
through two orders of development. Based upon a theory of change developed by Watzlawick, Weakland, and Fisch (1974), and Levinson's theory
(1978) of adult developmental stages, Terkelson's approach sees first-order
developments as experienced by family members as related to adaptation
and mastery but requiring no major alteration in personal identity. Second-

order developments, in contrast, involve transformation of status and meaning and require major alterations in family structure as well. Awareness of bisexuality or homosexuality in a family member represents a second-order change. Structural transformation is required from the family in order to validate development in the sexually variant individual and to functionally incorporate the reciprocal behaviors of other family members. The goal of family therapy, as always, is to enable the dysfunctional family to once again support developmentally appropriate need attainment in all family members.

Intervention may include the provision of information, values clarification, facilitation of communication, development of extrafamilial support systems, and (Bowenian) coaching. For example, when a spouse signals by his or her behavior a change in or a realization of his or her bisexuality or homosexuality, a functional system will respond by acknowledging that change in some overt manner. Symptoms, however, appear in a family member when the family has not made the shifts in structure required by this second-order developmental change. Subsequently, the index (symptomatic) member may seek treatment for anxiety, depression, alcohol or other chemical dependency; may obtain marital counseling or sex therapy; or may develop physical complaints and seek medical treatment. If the index member is a child, he or she may exhibit developmental or behavioral problems.

As noted previously, the bisexual or homosexual family member may be unaware of his or her sexual orientation, may be aware but feel confused about it, or may be fully aware but not have disclosed it to other family members. Regardless, when the sexual practices of a member are a family secret, there will be attendant stresses. It also is common for a partner to have "come out" to his or her spouse or to the extended family with the result that one or more members enter therapy as a strategy to "fix" the sexual orientation or modify the sexual practices of the variant member.

The identification of bisexuality or homosexuality in a family member is usually experienced as a crisis. It represents a discordant shift in familial role identities, an alteration of images of self and others, and a dissolution of major portions of one's expectable environment. In addition, it may represent a formidable assault upon deeply held social values, including cherished religious beliefs.

Once the crisis of initial revelation is past, the ability of families to accept differences and to support subsequent developmental and behavioral sequelae is related to the degree of individuation within the family and to the attendant ability to separate thinking and feeling (Kerr, 1981).

TREATMENT ISSUES

Family Functioning

Pressures for second-order change, such as with the emergence of bisexuality or homosexuality in a family member, may become evident in less specifically sexual but more pragmatic problems of family operation. In working with mixed-orientation couples, it is useful for the family therapist to recognize some of the common signals of family dysfunction and to be able to support family members as they find solutions to these problems. Each member is encouraged to identify and express his or her own thoughts and feelings and to communicate those clearly to other family members. This facilitates the individuation of each person, while concomitantly considering the reality of the family's current situation. The misuse of alcohol and other drugs, for example, may represent system members' attempts at self-medication in the face of system-induced anxiety or depression. The misuse of money by either partner may be taken as a signal of system dysfunction as well. Therapists have found that sessions devoted to discerning the process of financial planning and management may bring to light other dysfunctional behaviors and enable the family to experience successful problem solving, while somewhat defusing sexual issues.

Parenting

The central bond in a mixed-orientation relationship is often organized around parenting, e.g., mutual pleasure in the children and the individual satisfactions each partner derives from parenting tasks and interaction with children.

Even following disclosure—because of the lack of a socially approved role model for homosexual parenting, as well as fears of social ostracism for both partners, and concern over burdening their children with a damaged sociosexual identity—partners may choose to remain stuck in dysfunctional chaos rather than move toward resolving second-order change by fully acknowledging the actual nature of their relationship. This immobility may be signaled through symptoms in the children, anxiety or depression in either parent, or by any member of the family distancing from it and reattaching to some extrafamilial group or person. Indeed, one parent may abandon the parenting role almost entirely.

To effectively assist family members in confronting their immobility and progressing toward functional family solutions, the therapist needs to provide family members with information that will broaden the scope of members' alternatives and will permit them to make choices that allow them to meet their personal needs while resuming a "good enough" parent-child interaction. Gay and lesbian support networks, knowledgeable helping professionals, local or national rap lines, informed media presentations, and sympathetic clergy may provide both therapist and family members with such useful information. Clearly, work with mixed-orientation couples requires that the therapist remain current with regard to research on a wide range of sexual issues.

Disclosure

Where sexual orientation has become a family secret, as is often initially the case with mixed-orientation couples seen in therapy, the process of disclosure is different from a more usual developmental sorting out. Still, the family therapist can utilize the same concepts and methods that he or she would use for the disclosure of any other family secret and can expect to see many of the same phenomena. For example, there may be signals from the partner who is bisexual or homosexual, such as a shift to an age-inappropriate style of dress, with concomitant avoidance or denial of such signals from the other partner. Other covert disclosure patterns include a low level of sexual energy expressed between the partners, or one partner being involved with friendship groups of dramatically different age or interests from those encountered in the social life of the couple. Still other couples may experience high levels of sexual interaction for short periods, with a resumption of a relatively asexual relationship between those periods. Such times of high activity may coincide with homosexual activity or with its absence. It is the change in the level of activity or in a well-established pattern of behavior that is important.

It is useful to have an agreement with the family or couple that any material revealed in an individual session that is relevant for therapy will be expressed in the joint sessions by that individual, with the support of the therapist. Such a contract precludes the therapist from prematurely gaining access to a family secret and needing to deal with it in a way that interferes with the ongoing flow of therapy. Some couples will be able to disclose in their own place and time, but not within the session, while others, who find it more anxiety producing, may seek the support of the therapist. Ordinarily, once the "secret" has been expressed, there is a reduction in anxiety and rapid forward movement in the therapy.

Disclosure to children of adult sexual orientation is a process that is dealt with in an individualized way, depending upon the couple's values and family system's rules, as well as the developmental stage of each child. Children in American society usually are not informed of the details of their parents' sexual behavior. A more appropriate time to discuss these matters is when children raise relevant questions or when life-style changes are in place. The couple who express a need to go into detail concerning their sexual life style may be helped to explore the intent or purpose of such disclosure. They may be inappropriately looking for intrafamilial support, reinforcement, or guilt reduction through approval by their children. In addition, disclosure may lead to subtle attempts by one or both parents to encourage children to take sides. Such approaches fail to provide functional ways for children to deal with their parents' sexuality. In short, the family may need help in working through these issues of disclosure intent and style.

Parents frequently turn to the therapist for advice concerning the timing and content of disclosure. These decisions are basically the responsibility of the parents. The therapist, as coach, can help them consider the developmental tasks and vulnerabilities of each child and to assess the possible impact of such information. None of these considerations negates the importance of a general discussion of the social implications of a sexually variant life style. These are likely to be of particular interest to adolescents, given their considerable concern about sexuality in general. Such issues, especially if they are raised by the children, constitute a legitimate area of family informational exchange. Children and adolescents in families need information about issues that will impinge upon their ways of understanding their own lives or that are likely to relate to changes in their lives (whether it is place of residence, who will be parenting them, or who might be the significant others entering the family network). Questions not related to these issues usually may be considered as relating to the needs of the adults within the system and not those of the children.

Disclosure must be placed within the psychosocial developmental framework of both parents and children. Is the bisexual or homosexual parent 49 and the child in his or her late 20s? Is the parent 21 and the child 2? Is the adolescent 13 or 19? As always, therapy must meet the family system and its components as they are.

Sexual Awareness

Education in human sexuality is an important aspect of therapy for mixed-orientation couples, as it provides an opportunity for each partner to better understand his or her own feelings and behavior. It also fosters understanding of one's partner's behavior and feelings. Even though the couple may seem sophisticated, the therapist should not assume that they possess a thorough understanding of sexuality. The importance of a thorough sexual history that includes facts, attitudes, and behavior becomes obvious at the point at which bisexuality or homosexuality is brought forth as an issue in therapy.

It may be useful to have individual sessions in which either partner feels safe enough to risk revealing his or her sexual naiveté. These sessions provide an opportunity for the client to ask questions specifically relating to bisexual or homosexual practices, sexually transmitted diseases, and implications of various life-style choices. Specifically, in relation to sexually transmitted diseases, it is helpful to have available for purposes of referral male and female physicians who are competent and willing to treat patients with sexually variant life styles. Physician comfort with bisexuality and homosexuality is particularly important since patients often are especially sensitive to any signs of homophobia or other value judgments during this time of personal and familial transition. For the couple's own protection, the topic of sexually transmitted diseases must be discussed. For the heterosexual partner, an unwillingness to discuss this issue may represent continued efforts to resist second-order system change around his or her partner's sexual behavior, i.e., an attempt to maintain the status quo. Similarly, an unwillingness to discuss this area of the relationship may represent an attempt by the bisexual or homosexual partner to trivialize the impact of his or her sexual behavior upon the family system.

Sexual Scripts

For those mixed-orientation couples who choose to maintain the relationship, there are few models or rules upon which to base its functioning. In this regard, the sociosexual scripts (sexual value systems) of the system members are of extreme importance, since such scripts enable interaction to occur by providing a program or strategy of action along with reasons for engaging in the activity (Gecas & Libby, 1976). Assessment of sexual scripts would involve each client reviewing script elements emanating from different reference groups and value positions. However, this can contribute to the existing system anxiety as the questions are considered—whether or not, for example, one should adhere to the religious script developed in one's family of origin or the recreational script of one's peer group. The relevance of sociosexual scripts is that they provide major elements of the family system members' orientation toward sexual activity and must be considered highly influential in defining the context within which sexual arousal and specific behavior is judged "good," "bad," "fun," "dirty," "acceptable," and so on. In the analysis of sexual scripts, transactional analysis techniques aimed at eliciting parent messages and life script decisions can lead to client awareness of early sexual decisions. It is then possible for the client to examine current choices and to make informed decisions based upon present data.

By using the protective clinical environment for such an assessment, each person is better able to think about the implications of his or her own sexual scripting. Each also is better able to listen with acceptance to the other's sexual imperatives. As understanding increases, each can develop modifications in his or her own sexual script that lead toward continuing mutuality, as befits the couple's initial objective of maintaining their mixed-orientation relationship.

However, the decision to remain together, with a successful accommodation of both partners' scripts, is less likely than a decision to separate. Still, script assessment may be useful in providing information that clients can use to consider relationship choices in a more rational, less emotionally reactive way.

A TREATMENT MODEL

The therapist's ability to remain objective in the presence of emotionally valenced sexual issues that have emerged in therapy is crucial if clients are to resolve their developmental impasse. The assumption of an advocacy position in the direction of encouraging sexual experimentation, or of labeling the mixed-orientation relationship pathological per se is to be avoided. An advocacy position inevitably results in the perception that the therapist is biased. This may lead the client to feel attacked and to drop out of treatment.

Useful treatment goals with mixed-orientation couples are the reduction of anxiety within the system and the facilitation of individuation in its members. Through the attainment of such goals, the couple is able to proceed with problem solving, based upon their own needs and values. Specifically, provision of information is an important element in the treatment of the mixed-orientation couple. As the family members learn concepts of family systems theory, they are able to begin to think about the developmental process and the interrelationships that have previously only been experienced at an emotional level. Individuals begin to understand life patterns, purpose, and outcome as they gain information and knowledge about their own sexuality, human developmental tasks, the family life cycle, and other sociocultural and sociosexual models of family living. These goals are met through the sequential utilization of the therapist's treatment skills, knowledge of family systems theory, and understanding of human sexuality.

A contract for change with each client is an effective tool. One partner typically identifies objectives that lead to emotional distancing, while the other typically looks for ways to adapt or cling. Though contracts for each may or may not be congruent, the therapist affirms the goals established by each and supports plans of action. Following the establishment of contracts and during subsequent sessions, the therapist encourages clients to evaluate the ways in which they meet or avoid their self-defined goals for change. Through this process, clients become aware of the personal and familial impact of their choices. They are able to expand their range of options in given situations through the contracting process, with a concomitant reduction in their anxiety.

The availability of supervision or consultation is important even to the experienced therapist who treats families in which bisexuality or homosexuality of one of the marital partners has emerged as an issue. The therapist is becoming inducted into the system when he or she loses sight of the direction of therapy, begins to label one partner victim and the other persecutor, begins to function as a rescuer out of the perception that one partner is in some way abused or powerless, or engages in denial and intellectualization of the issue of bisexuality or homosexuality. Feelings of voyeuristic titillation or moralistic condemnation also indicate that the therapist has failed to remain therapeutically differentiated.

The option of whether to refer or to invite in a co-therapist when sexual material emerges is in part determined by the therapist's own comfort with and knowledge of sexually variant behavior, attitudes, and lifestyles. If the choice is made to refer, it is of great importance that the family understand the basis upon which the referral is made. Once a therapeutic bond has been established with a family, the preferable choice for the therapist who is uninformed about nontraditional sexual lifestyles may be to acquire information and supervision, sufficient to allow him or her to remain in a therapeutic stance.

Many of the challenges faced by the family therapist treating mixed-orientation couples are illustrated by the case of Kurt and Astrid Halverson (not the couple's real identity).

Kurt phoned for an appointment, but refused to be seen with Astrid. The therapist had requested that both come. Kurt defined his problems as career dissatisfaction, relationship difficulties throughout his extended family, and an unsatisfactory sex life with Astrid. This dissatisfaction had persisted for 8 years, with sexual abstinence (within the marriage) characterizing the preceding year. He attributed his personal feelings of sexual guilt and confusion to a strict religious upbringing. Kurt wanted individual therapy for himself, but also hoped that Astrid would seek help and change so that he could enjoy his marriage to her. He informed Astrid that he was getting therapy and encouraged her to do the same, and she immediately contacted the therapist. Astrid saw her problems as a lack of intimacy in her marriage, sexual deprivation, and a feeling that "There must be something wrong with me because I am unable to please my husband." Both partners were committed to their marriage of some 15 years, and both enjoyed being parents of their three boys, Lars (13), Peter (12), and Adrian (7).

Kurt began psychodynamic group treatment, while Astrid was seen for individual psychotherapy. It was hoped that Kurt would soon join Astrid for conjoint treatment. Astrid contracted to identify and to deal with her part of the couple's marital problems, while Kurt contracted to confront and resolve his sexual confusion and to claim and express authentic emotions. After 10 months of once-weekly sessions in this mode of treatment, individuation had progressed to the point where Kurt requested conjoint sessions in order to confront and resolve the continuing marital impasse. Astrid welcomed this. Specifically, Kurt's goals for the conjoint sessions were to identify blocks to sexual intercourse with Astrid. Her goal for conjoint therapy was to increase her range of choices in interacting with Kurt. Both agreed upon the goal of also developing nonsexual, positive ways of being together. At this point, Astrid also entered group treatment with the goal of learning to think rather than simply making reactive, "parental" responses to Kurt and others. Kurt's group goal now became the replacement of adaptive responses with authentic ones. It should be pointed out that Kurt and Astrid were assigned separate groups.

The next six conjoint sessions were very productive for the Halversons. Each partner was able to stay individuated and to hear the other. The sexual script of each was reviewed. During these sessions, Astrid shared with Kurt and the therapist the family secret of her premarital pregnancy by another man. This disclosure helped both to understand Astrid's initial wish to have a gentle, accepting marital relationship with no sexual demands. It also allowed Kurt to understand that the marriage problems had been mutually evolved and that the current impasse was not entirely the result of his sexual confusion.

The shift in the system from a position of self-blame to one in which each member perceived the shared nature of past relationship decisions allowed Kurt to raise the issue of his bisexual and homosexual feelings and behavior. This precipitated a crisis that soon rippled throughout the extended family system and resulted in much turmoil for a period of about a month. Moreover, Kurt and Astrid's discomfort with the inclusion of this new information into the family system led to a shift away from their focus in therapy. This they accomplished by beginning to discuss previously unmentioned concerns regarding their children. For example, one concern was withdrawing behavior in Peter (12), with an accompanying drop in his school performance; the other was the revelation to the therapist that Adrian (7) had been encopretic throughout the course of therapy. Kurt and Astrid had disagreed about the need to obtain help for him from the therapist. Both children responded positively to individual therapy by child psychiatry colleagues.

Following effective treatment of the children, the couple were able to return to their work with what was clearly a mixed-orientation marriage. By now, fortunately, they were able to communicate effectively. Their first self-defined goal was to evolve a new relationship structure, i.e., a sexually open marriage. However, as they worked toward this, both Astrid and Kurt learned that the value system and the family life style that such a relationship necessitated violated their own values and beliefs to an intolerable degree. It was at this point that they decided to separate. Even so, both remained focused upon parenting issues and consequently were able to develop a clear and mutually acceptable parenting contract.

The issue of whether or not to disclose to extended family members the sexual aspects of their reasons for divorce was the focus of several subsequent sessions. The children were confused as to why their parents were divorcing in the light of their now amiable relationship. The case was terminated with a series of four family sessions that allowed the parents to feel more confident that each child's needs were being met, while at the same time better meeting their own recently acknowledged needs. Questions of specific sexual practices did not arise. In these last sessions, there was an open discussion of newly defined family structure. Each person was able to clarify his or her place in this structure and to affirm positive connections to every other family member.

In addition to the other points made above, the preceding case example emphasizes that (1) the presenting problem is not necessarily clearly related to bisexual or homosexual issues, especially as disclosed to the therapist by the client; (2) while there are pure models of family therapy, when working with mixed-orientation couples and their extended families, a flexible approach such as that presented may facilitate therapeutic movement; (3) contracting facilitates individuation and keeps the clients in charge of the timing of their changes and disclosures. Finally, even though a therapist works from a family systems approach, it often is pragmatically necessary to begin with individuals or other system segments. Such an approach can be conceptualized within a family systems model and allows the therapist to persist in moving toward the inclusion of more system members as this becomes clinically possible, i.e., as the members become willing to participate actively in therapy.

The utilization of the family system model in the treatment of mixed-orientation couples and their families is an effective way to support each member's development and to enable the family to continue to meet the needs of its individual members.

ADOLESCENTS AND THEIR FAMILIES

The family therapist, especially one in a child- and family-focused agency, usually sees family concerns about homosexuality from the perspective of parental questions about "effeminate" mannerisms or other behavior patterns in sons that do not fit the family model of appropriate masculinity. Parents are much less likely to become alarmed over gender-discrepant interests and behaviors in girls. Given the double-standard socialization process through which females develop, one that holds female sexuality to be less powerful than male sexuality, the close association of young women in same-sex living arrangements, all-girl sports, and same-sex "socializing" groups is viewed with greater tolerance and less suspicion than is the case for men. Male adolescents also are seen more frequently with respect to issues of bisexuality and homosexuality because of their greater tendency to manifest gender-discrepant behavior and affectional responses at an earlier age and because of the higher proportion of male to female homosexuals of any age in the general population (Bell, Weinberg, & Hammersmith, 1981). On the other hand, an adolescent who is clear about his or her sexual preference may be brought for treatment by parents seeking to effect some change or "normalization" of the child. Or an adolescent may individually initiate therapy because of sexual confusion or panic.

A solid base of information regarding child development and current information on bisexuality and homosexuality are indispensable to the therapist in this setting. Adequate evaluation may also require psychological testing or the assessment of the teen-ager by a competent and nonprejudiced child psychiatrist. A developmentally oriented and nonrejecting therapeutic stance allows a child the opportunity for expression and exploration and still avoids a premature labeling of sexual orientation.

Teen-agers and their parents are more aware of bisexuality and homosexuality today. Indeed, in some instances they are hypersensitive and may become alarmed when developmentally expected same-sex interests occur in early adolescence. They may benefit from information and reassurance. However, if an adolescent self-identifies as gay or lesbian, and if professional evaluation supports that identification, then the family therapist must address the developmental needs of the individual and those of the family system. While the self-identified gay or lesbian adolescent has the same developmental tasks as his or her heterosexual peers, the prevailing societal value system makes it difficult for the adolescent who is confused about sexual identity, or who proclaims a bisexual or homosexual identity, to experiment with adult roles and to experience normative social behaviors and associated sexual affectional relationships within the matrix of the family system. The heterosexual teen utilizes such experiences and exploration in ways that allow him or her to enter adulthood with confidence and competence. The gay or lesbian teen, because of the restrictive sociofamilial context in which he or she lives, often must postpone this adolescent process.

Adolescent Behaviors

The gay or lesbian teen may appear in the clinician's office as depressed or withdrawn. He or she also may express feelings of self-hatred and associated guilt. Yet another pattern is the defiance of familial and social norms in such a way as to provoke a family crisis. Much of this behavior is determined by or is in reaction to family culture; i.e., expectations of what it means to be an adult male or female (gender expectations); what it means to be a Catholic, Protestant, or Jewish adult male or female (religious expectations), etc. Such expectational parameters to a considerable degree also define the family's tolerance of diversity or deviance within its own boundaries.

Parental Responses

When confronted with the disclosure or discovery of their son's or daughter's gay or lesbian orientation, parents may react with anger, confusion, blame, guilt, or desperation. From the time of conception, they have had an image of their child's future identity. Typically, they foresee a daughter or son getting married, and themselves becoming grandparents. They see the child becoming more or less successful in more or less conventional ways and leading a more or less socially conventional life. The discordant news that one of their offspring is gay or lesbian, or might "become one," often quickly and painfully destroys those dreams, if not in all ways for all time at least initially for the majority of parents.

Therapists are faced with parents who need help in assuaging their anguish, reducing their guilt, and in finding understanding in the place of blame. In a fundamental way, therapists are faced with the task of helping families remake their myths, of helping them restructure the meaning of being parents, by incorporating new and unwelcome information. The alternative seems to be a situation in which overt or subterranean recriminations fly fast and furious. The father may be castigated for being too remote or passive with the son or for encouraging the daughter to play baseball or go out for track. The mother may be ridiculed for allowing the son to play with dolls or for permitting the daughter to become a tomboy. One of the problems with such recrimination is that it is very easy for the gay or lesbian (or undecided but experimenting) adolescent to assume that he or she is bad enough or powerful enough to be responsible for the pain his or her parents obviously are feeling.

Recrimination also tends to polarize meaning and to facilitate the image that the adolescent is either all bad or all good. The danger here is that this may short-circuit the teen's own process of consideration of a gay or lesbian life style by forcing him or her to balance the "all bad" self-image formed in reference to the parents' reactions with an "everything is great" image of gay or lesbian life styles. Such polarization impedes the continued development of the gay or lesbian individual, as it also blocks family maturation. Both long-term recrimination and the festering sore of denial bind tremendous familial energy to individual members' experience and expression of anxiety and depression.

Treatment Issues

The adolescent who comes into therapy with concerns about his or her own bisexuality or homosexuality offers the family therapist a unique challenge in that there is often little professional consensus as to what constitutes appropriate therapy. For example, depending upon the colleagues one chooses to use as members of an evaluation and treatment team, one may well get strong differences of opinion about the "correct" approach and the manner in which whatever material is presented is to be interpreted. However, differences in perspective, if welcomed by the therapist, can prove an invaluable source of information. From the perspective of the family therapist who is developmentally based, a conservative, as opposed to an extreme, position that allows the adolescent to explore his or her sexuality within the context of the family, peer relationships, and general social environment seems to offer the greatest chance for an authentic integration of the adolescent's own sexual orientation. This stance also tends to minimize the tendency the client might have to prematurely label affectional responses or behavior on the one hand, or to engage in rebellious resistance, on the other. In those instances the adolescent assumes a public position without the benefit of a thorough exploration of its implications or of continued developmental growth. The approach we are proposing allows the adolescent needed time to explore the nonsexual aspects of what may at first appear to be primarily a sexual issue. It encourages the social and intellectual development of the adolescent, as well as that of sexual discovery, without taking an advocacy position.

Parents faced with an adolescent who either is confused about his or her sexual orientation or who is insistent that he or she is gay, lesbian, or bisexual present a slightly different set of treatment issues. The family may well appear to be deeply concerned or overtly angry at the teen-ager (index member). Parents and other family members will need information and the therapist's support to tolerate the adolescent's exploration without forcing him or her into some personally inappropriate position. During this exploratory phase, full-fledged parental participation in support groups for parents of bisexuals and homosexuals is usually contraindicated, unless the orientation of the adolescent is crystal clear to all concerned, since this participation may constitute additional pressure to prematurely label and to thwart the process of exploration. Nonetheless, it is always a useful adjunct to therapy for parents to know of such support groups and to utilize their resources when appropriate.

Proceeding with Treatment

The first phase in working with the adolescent is to obtain a thorough physical and psychological assessment, which also may include child psychiatric evaluation. However, it is crucial that the client not perceive this as part of a pathological labeling process. This requires great sensitivity and considerable negotiation from the therapist, not only with the adolescent himself or herself, but also with the extended family. It further requires that the therapist carefully select colleagues competent and willing to work with teens regarding sexual issues. An additional rationale for this type of assessment is that the adolescent may initially come into treatment with symptoms of anxiety, depression, or acting-out behavior, rather than overtly raising questions about his or her sexual orientation. Consequently, a thorough workup may begin to uncover underlying sexual concerns and help the therapist in working with the family system toward getting these sexual concerns into therapy where they can be resolved.

It also may be useful to utilize teen support groups as an adjunct to therapy. Any such group should not be identified as a bisexual or homosexual support group, but rather should be structured to provide information on and permission to discuss all aspects of adolescent sexuality. Moreover, any such group should be developmentally segregated so that the young teen is differentiated from one who is older and who is likely to be closer to a more clearly established sexual identity. While permission to gain information and to check out sexual issues with peers is a primary function of any such group, of equal importance is the opportunity to discuss the nature of relationships, and the implications of life-style choices. It is of fundamental importance that the person or persons providing the leadership be competent both in the specific topics that are likely to emerge as well as in the skills of being a group therapist.

The family therapist working with families with a bisexual or homosexual child needs to stay constantly aware of the adjunct services that are beginning to become available. And while the current knowledge base is complex and often unclear as to which factors (e.g., prenatal biological, psychodynamic, or social) influence the sexual orientation of any one person, at a minimum the therapist can help families understand that should one of their adolescent members be gay, lesbian, or bisexual, blame and self-blame are useless, while working through the meanings of that orientation to the family as a whole may be beneficial to all. Work with families that have a bisexual or homosexual adolescent member parallels work with mixed-orientation couples in that movement is toward differentiation within the family system in a manner that avoids emotional cutoffs while allowing for normal developmental progression.

REFERENCES

Bayer, R. *Homosexuality and American psychiatry: The politics of diagnosis*. New York: Basic Books, 1981.

Bell, A.P., Weinberg, M.S., & Hammersmith, S.K. *Sexual preference: Its development in men and women*. Bloomington: Indiana University Press, 1981.

Gecas, V., & Libby, R. Sexual behavior as symbolic interaction. *The Journal of Sex Research,* 1976, *12,* 33-49.

Hooker, E. Parental relations and male homosexuality in patient and nonpatient samples. *Journal of Consulting and Clinical Psychology,* 1969, *33,* 140-142.

Kerr, M. Family systems theory and therapy. In A. Gurman & D. Kniskern (Eds.), *Handbook of family therapy.* New York: Brunner/Mazel, 1981.

Levinson, D.J., Darrow, C.N., Klein, E.B., Levinson, M.H., & McKee, B. *The seasons of a man's life.* New York: Knopf, 1978.

Rifkin, H.A. Homosexuality in marriage. In E.S. Rosenbaum & I. Alger (Eds.), *The marriage relationship.* New York: Basic Books, 1968.

Robinson, B.E., Skeen, P., Hobson, C.F., & Herrman, M. Gay men's and women's perceptions of early family life and their relationships with parents. *Family Relations,* 1982, *31,* 79-83.

Ross, H.L. Odd couples: Homosexuals in heterosexual marriages. *Sexual Behavior,* July 1972, pp. 42-50.

Saghir, T., & Robins, E. *Male and female homosexuality.* Baltimore: Williams and Wilkins, 1973.

Terkelsen, K.G. Toward a theory of the family life cycle. In E.A. Carter & M. McGoldrick (Eds.), *The family life cycle: A framework for family therapy.* New York: Gardner Press, 1980.

Voeller, B., & Walters, J. Gay fathers. *The Family Coordinator,* April 1978, pp. 153-155.

Warren, C.A.B. Women among men: Females in the male homosexual community. *Archives of Sexual Behavior,* 1976, *5,* 166-167.

Watzlawick, P., Weakland, J.H., & Fisch, R. *Change: Principles of problem formation and problem resolution.* New York: Norton, 1974.

6. Incest and Sexual Violence

Karen Authier, MSW, ACSW
Assistant Professor of Psychiatric
    Social Work
College of Medicine
University of Nebraska at Omaha
Nebraska Psychiatric Institute
Omaha, Nebraska

Rhett Butler sweeps a struggling Scarlett O'Hara into his arms and ascends the grand plantation staircase. Although *Gone With the Wind* lacked explicit portrayal of sexual activity, there was little doubt in the moviegoer's mind that sex occurred. The details of the sexual activities were left to the imagination. Was it seduction or spousal rape? Certainly, the writer, director, and actress portrayed a rapturous Scarlett the next morning. In reality, the aura surrounding forced sex, within or outside of marriage, encountered by the family therapist lacks any semblance of romance in comparison.

In another book-into-movie classic, *Lolita,* the theme of the eternal romantic triangle is embellished by the portrayal of a seductive youngster who enters into a sexual liaison with her stepfather to the exclusion of her mother. "Lolita" has become a synonym for a sexually precocious and seductive young girl. The implied blame directed toward the character Lolita and other "Lolitas" in thousands of other sexually abusive families is a continuing phenomenon encountered by practitioners who work with those families.

SEXUAL ABUSE AND THE FAMILY THERAPIST

As in the arts, sexual issues are frequently important in therapy. While most therapists view sexuality as a positive channel of human expression and often identify their role as assisting individuals or couples to enhance their sexual functioning, sometimes therapists encounter types of sexual behavior and sexual experiences that not only are dysfunctional, but also have destructive impact on individuals and families. Far from serving as a positive channel of human expression, sexual behavior can be abusive, exploitive, violent, and assaultive.

In this article, the term "sexual abuse" will include all situations in which an individual is engaged in any type of sexual activity without his or her consent because of coercion, intimidation, or the belief that he or she cannot refuse. Included in this definition are any forms of sexual activity between a child and an adult with the assumption that a child lacks the ability for informed consent and defers to the power of the adult even without actual threat or use of physical force. For both children and adults, male and female, the definition includes sexual misuse by someone known or un-known to the victim, within or outside the victim's family. The term "sexual assault" will be used for those sexual abuse situations where violence or the threat of violence is used by the attacker. Although "rape" is a term commonly used as a synonym for sexual assault, rape is more narrowly defined, by law and in strict usage, as forced intercourse and sometimes excludes homosexual assault. Since sexual abuse can be heterosexual or homosexual and can include a variety of types of sexual activity, the broader term of "sexual abuse" is preferred for this discussion.

This article will examine sexual abuse within the framework of family theory and family therapy. The family therapist may uncover sexual abuse as an issue during the course of treatment or may be presented with the issue of sexual abuse as a reason for the request for treatment. The sexual abuse may be current and ongoing or it may be an unresolved facet of a family member's past. The skilled therapist can also function in a preventive role by identifying "at risk" situations and using a preventive approach in the treatment process.

Intervention and treatment where sexual abuse is an issue should be family focused unless an individual is truly without a family. Even in situations in which family members are not available or willing to be involved in the treatment process, as we shall see, the therapist can maintain a family focus. Family sessions with the entire family unit present may be contraindicated in some cases. However, as family therapists increasingly recognize, the use of a family therapy approach does not require the physical presence of all family members at each session. Treatment can rely on a family approach even when only one family member is available.

There are multiple reasons for stressing the importance of a family approach in intervention with sexual abuse situations. Foremost is the premise that the family is an interactional system that affects and is affected by the distress and behavior of individual members. As Green (1981) concludes: "psychological distress cannot be understood separate from the social context of which it is a part. Psychological distress is part of trans-actional distress" (p. 32). The sexual misuse of a member causes reverberations within the family system, and the response of family members helps shape the reaction and the adjustment of the victim to the abuse. Sexual abuse by someone outside the family precipitates a crisis for the family as well as the victim; therefore, family-focused intervention is necessary. When sexual abuse occurs within the family, a family focus to intervention and treatment is essential, although family therapy may not be the initial treatment of choice.

Since the early 1970s, there has been increased interest and concern regarding the victims of sexual abuse and assault. This parallels an increase in the numbers of rapes appearing in the crime statistics, an increase in reports of child sexual abuse, and the development of a strong feminist movement. The increased interest is demonstrated by a proliferation of counseling programs for victims and the addition to the literature of books and articles dealing with sexual abuse. Awareness of those findings, combined with their knowledge base of family systems and their therapeutic "tricks of the trade" can provide family therapists with a sound foundation to approach intervention with cases of sexual abuse.

TYPES OF SEXUAL ABUSE

There seems to be a natural distinction between two types of sexual abuse: sexual abuse where the perpetrator is not a member of the victim's family and sexual abuse where the perpetrator is a member of the victim's family. Treatment considerations differ considerably with the two types of situations and each will be examined separately. Within those categories further distinction can be made between sexual abuse of adults and sexual abuse of children.

Much of the literature on victim response to sexual abuse derives from work with victims in programs such as rape crisis centers. The literature distinguishes various forms of sexual abuse, taking into account also the fact that the type of abuse is a variable that affects the victim's and the family's emotional management of the assault. Burgess and Holmstrom (1974) identify three basic categories of sexual victimization: (1) rape: sex without the victim's consent; (2) accessory-to-sex: inability to consent; and (3) sex-stress situations: sex with initial consent. They further divide those categories into subtypes.

Rape as sex without the victim's consent can be experienced as a blitz rape or confidence rape (Burgess & Holmstrom, 1974). The first subtype, blitz rape, probably would coincide most closely with what the general public and even some professionals would regard as "real rape." The victim is attacked and forced without his or her consent to engage in sexual activity, most frequently vaginal or anal intercourse or fellatio. A blitz rapist relies on surprise and force, e.g., the victim walking down a street is assaulted by a man who jumps out of the bushes or the woman returns from her apartment house laundry room to be assaulted by a stranger who has entered while she is gone.

In a confidence rape, the second subtype, the victim generally is enticed into trusting the assailant, who may even be known to the victim, and then is forced to engage in sexual activity (Burgess & Holmstrom, 1974). For instance, a woman having car trouble accepts a ride from a helpful stranger or even an acquaintance and then is driven to a secluded location and assaulted. Another example would be a woman who accepts an offer from a friend of her husband's to make a minor home repair while her husband is out of town and is then assaulted by the man. There is also the classic situation of a stranger enticing a child into his car for sexual purposes. However, contrary to that stereotype of child sexual abuse, the person victimizing a child is more frequently someone known to and trusted by the child, who uses the relationship to gain access to the child (DeFrancis, 1969). In some situations, the abuse may even occur over a period of time if the victim is too fearful to report the abuse. For instance, a young man accepted the offer of an acquaintance to "stop by for a beer" and was sodomized and beaten at knifepoint, but was too embarrassed to report the assault. His assailant used his victim's fear of embarrassment and threats of violence to continue the abuse over a period of several weeks until the victim finally mustered his courage to obtain assistance.

The second category of victimization (accessory-to-sex: inability to consent) includes all situations in which individuals agree to engage in sexual activity with some willingness but are sexually misused because they lack the ability to provide informed consent because of their age or mental incapacity (Burgess & Holmstrom, 1974). While most accessory-to-sex situations involve minors, there are some situations in which mentally retarded or psychotic adults are sexually misused or exploited by others. The following case provides an example.

A 19-year-old young woman who was assessed clinically as having borderline personality and borderline intelligence had been sexually abused since childhood by a brutal father. When her plight was discovered after an investigation into a report of the sexual abuse of a younger sister, she was offered assistance and aid in leaving the sexually abusive family home. The young woman discussed with a therapist her dislike of the sexual relationship with her father, but refused to leave the home. The reasons for her refusal were clearly embedded in the pathology of the enmeshed family system, which supported a passive mother/wife who was frequently hospitalized with a diagnosis of chronic schizophrenia; an antisocial, sadistic father/husband who was sexually and physically abusive; and children who had not been allowed to individuate and who also had become symptomatic. The outside systems were unable to exert sufficient pressure on the family to engage the powerful father and the family was able to defend itself against change—at least until the next crisis.

The general public, some professionals, and family members often respond to the third category (sex-stress situation: sex with initial consent) with a "well, you asked for it" attitude. In sex-stress situations the victim agrees to have sex, either for or without remuneration, but becomes a victim when the sexual partner goes beyond the bounds of the initial implied or explicit contract, for instance, by becoming violent or by forcing a type of sexual activity to which the victim objects (Burgess & Holmstrom, 1974). Prostitutes sometimes find themselves victims in this category. While some might argue that sex-stress abuse is an occupational hazard that prostitutes must accept, others, particularly feminists, deplore the callous attitudes with which these victims often are treated by law enforcement and people in the "helping professions."

Abuse by Someone outside the Family System

There have been several variations in the conceptualization of post-assault phases of response by the victim that are relevant to work with individuals abused by someone outside the family system. Most relate to some degree to crisis theory, although there is no clear indication that the originators used the literature on crisis theory to develop their conceptualizations. An early article by Fox and Scherl (1972) delineated a three-stage victim response: (1) acute reaction, (2) outward adjustment, and (3) integration and resolution of the experience. The authors are nonspecific regarding the types of emotional reactions victims present in Stage 1, but stress that there are practical as well as emotional aspects of the crisis, e.g., medical aspects, decisions regarding contacting law enforcement, and repair of or provision for home security. Stage 2 brings a lull in the response process, perhaps the calm before the storm that allows the victim some time to recoup emotional bearings. At this point the victim resists dealing actively with the memories of the assault. During Stage 3 there is a resurgence of emotionality, particularly depression, and victims are again willing to engage in therapeutic work toward resolution of their experience. In Fox and Scherl's small sample of previously well-adjusted young unmarried women, resolution occurred, seemingly without residual effects, in a relatively short period of time. Because of the methodological shortcomings, however, it would be unwise to generalize from that study.

Burgess and Holmstrom (1974), who completed a descriptive study of 146 victims admitted to a Boston emergency room with the complaint of rape, coined the phrase "rape trauma syndrome" to refer to the predictable symptoms and stages of response of the sexual assault victim. After the assault, the victim enters an acute phase, lasting several days to several weeks, which is characterized by disorganization; sleep disturbance; eating disturbance; physical complaints; mood swings; intensity of feelings including fear, shame, tearfulness, anger; and recurring thoughts of the assault. The second phase is the long-term reorganization process during which time the victim may continue to be symptomatic and may make changes such as moving or restricting activities. During this phase, dreams and nightmares may continue to be a problem, and phobias related to the assaultive experience may develop. Women may experience difficulty in heterosexual relationships, particularly with sexuality.

A subsequent, more sophisticated study by Kilpatrick, Resick, and Veronen (1981) found that most rape victims continue to have problems in functioning as a result of the rape 1 year after the assault. A study by McCahill, Meyer, and Fishman (1979) of 790 female sexual assault victims seen in a Philadelphia hospital emergency room between 1972 and 1975 found that from 17% to 65.9% of their sample, which included some children and adolescents, experienced difficulty in 13 specific problem areas immediately after the assault, with the percentages decreasing to a range of 15.2% to 54.1% at the 1-year follow-up assessment. The 13 problem areas in increasing order of frequency were worsened relations with the family, increased insecurities concerning sexual attractiveness, worsened relations with husband or boyfriend, increased nightmares, increased negative feelings toward known men, worsened heterosexual relationships, increased fear of being home alone, worsened sexual relationships with a partner, change in eating habits, change in sleeping patterns, decreased social activities, increased negative feelings toward unknown men, and increased fear of streets. The number of women reporting decreased social activities (50%) was the only category in which the problem showed an increase in frequency at the 1-year post-assault interview (58.6%). Slightly over one-fourth of the women reported worsened relations with husband or boyfriend immediately after the assault, and that percentage had decreased by only .9% at the 1-year post-assault interview. After 1 year over half of the subjects still reported problems in three areas: increased fear of streets; increased negative feelings toward unknown men; and decreased social activities.

Sexual assault on a member produces a crisis response for the family unit, which in many cases moves to a state of disequilibrium because it cannot resolve the distress caused by the assault through use of available problem-solving skills, behaviors, or resources. Tension in the family system rises and the family makes repeated attempts to reduce the tension and reestablish equilibrium. The application of family crisis theory to such situations is particularly relevant. Through application of crisis theory to family theory, therapists obtain a model for intervention with family units in the aftermath of the crisis of sexual assault.

Caplan's (1964) phases of crisis resolution were used initially to explain individual crisis response but are helpful in understanding family crisis response. The findings of Kilpatrick et al. (1981) also tend to substantiate the value of utilizing a crisis model in work with families of assault victims. Although their assessments focused on the response of the adult victims, not the family unit, their findings have important implications for therapy with the family. Assessment on various scales (depression, social adjustment, fear, anxiety, mood, and self-esteem) at intervals of 6 to 21 days, 1 month, 3 months, 6 months, and 1 year following the rape indicated that victims were significantly more symptomatic than a matched control at the 6- to 21-day and 1-month assessments, but that the victims' symptoms had decreased at the 3-month, 6-month, and 1-year post-rape assessments to the point that they differed significantly from the control group only in the areas of elevated fear and anxiety scores. Certainly, the reduction of symptoms by 3 months tends to support the theory of time-limited crisis response. The residual fear and anxiety indicate that some emotional effects of the rape linger after the crisis phase has passed. Results also seemed to suggest that some victims deteriorated slightly in functioning between the 6-month and 1-year assessments, although there was no statistical significance in those results. In a less sophisticated follow-up assessment of their original sample, Burgess and Holmstrom (1979) found that some victims believed that they still had not recovered from the assault after 5 years.

The evidence that, for many victims, difficulties linger does not in itself negate the application of crisis theory to sexual assault. Crisis theory posits only that there is a predictable time frame for crisis resolution. It recognizes the risk of negative resolution of the crisis, that is, stabilization of functioning at a level lower than pre-crisis functioning. Moreover, a complicating factor in applying the time frame of crisis theory to the crisis of sexual assault is that frequently the assault is merely the beginning, and not necessarily the most traumatic, of a string of crises for the victim. Additional crises or exacerbation of the initial crisis occur for some victims with the investigation by law enforcement, the filing of criminal charges, possible subsequent threats from the assailant or the assailant's friends or family, seeing the assailant or someone who looks like the assailant, and finally the court trial. In fact, some victims find the trial to be an experience as negative or even more negative than the assault (Burgess & Holmstrom, 1974, 1979; McCahill et al., 1979). The additional crises interfere with the victim's ability to achieve post-assault adjustment and complicate the treatment process.

Clearly the victim's post-assault symptoms described in the literature have potentially troublesome implications for the family unit. In addition to feeling the impact of the victim's reactions to the assault, the family itself is a variable affecting the post-assault adjustment of the victim. McCahill et al. (1979) found some correlation between the frequency of certain symptoms and the living arrangement of the victim. In their study, unmarried victims living with father, mother, sister, or brother experienced fewer post-assault problems than married victims living with husbands. This finding applied to the following: change in eating habits, change in sleeping patterns, increased nightmares, increased fear of being home alone, worsened heterosexual relationships, and insecurities concerning sexual attractiveness. Married women reported less satisfactory post-assault relationships with other family members (not including the husband) than unmarried women. More unmarried victims living with father-present families had positive feelings toward men they knew than other victims at the 1-year post-assault assessment. The assault experience had a more negative impact on victim-husband relationships for married women than for victim-boyfriend relationships for unmarried women.

The Philadelphia study (McCahill et al., 1979) also noted variables other than family situations that affected the post-assault adjustment of victims. In that study children and adolescents were less likely than adults to experience symptoms in the year following the assault. The investigators speculated on several possibilities. The fact that all children and adolescents in the sample lived with family members while some adults lived independent of family could account for that difference, because the study also found that victims living with family had fewer post-assault problems. The comparative lack of symptomatology during that first year does not, however, preclude delayed trauma reactions, such as delayed post-traumatic stress reactions. Another variable was history of behavioral/emotional problems. Victims whose behavior previously had involved them with the police were more likely to modify their social activities after the assault. Adjustment was more difficult for those victims with a history of emotional problems. In regard to employment status, there was a negative correlation between employment outside the home and positive post-assault adjustment, except in the area of quality of sexual relations. In that area, unemployed victims were less likely to experience deterioration in sexual relations with their partner.

Variables related to the assault itself also influenced post-assault adjustment. Assaults at two ends of a continuum posed greatest adjustment difficulties for victims: assaults that were especially brutal or undeniably life threatening and assaults that lacked substantial use of force or contained acts of counterfeit tenderness. Assault by a casual acquaintance more frequently led to fearfulness of being home alone than assault by a stranger. The victims' previous sexual experiences, beliefs, and values affected their response to various types of sexual activities endured during the assault. The location of the assault influenced the areas of adjustment that the victim found most difficult.

There is little scientific basis for generalization regarding the adjustment process for men and boys. While they may be less likely to be at risk for sexual assault than women and girls, it is also possible that men are even less likely than women to report or seek assistance after an assault. Those few men and boys who have happened into sexual assault studies seem to have responded to the assault in a manner similar to their female counterparts (Burgess & Holmstrom, 1974).

Abuse by Someone within the Family System

When the victim and the perpetrator of the abuse belong to the same family system, the complexity of the dynamics is greatly increased. The literature on intrafamily sexual abuse focuses almost exclusively on the abuse of children. Although there has been some increased attention to spousal rape, the literature on violence in the family has tended to ignore spousal rape as a component of domestic violence.

Spousal Rape

Few women take steps to report or obtain assistance subsequent to a rape by their husband, and the incidence of spousal rape remains unknown. Indeed, many women seem to believe they are not entitled to complain to any extent about forced sexual activity within the marriage relationship. The information about spousal rape is primarily anecdotal. For instance:

> A woman who was seen with her husband as a result of a school referral related to behavioral problems of one of the children described her husband as a "stubborn man." When asked by the therapist to provide an example of what that meant to her, she laughed nervously and provided as illustration that he was "so stubborn" that when she returned from the hospital after each of her deliveries he had insisted on resuming intercourse within a few days of the birth of each child despite her protests

and "broke my stitches." Further questions revealed that the timing and content of sexual activities were the exclusive prerogative of the husband. Generally, the wife submitted to her husband's requests, no matter how unreasonable they seemed to her. However, on those occasions following childbirth when she feared the pain and physical consequences of intercourse, she did assert herself and tried to resist her husband's demands. The result was spousal rape. The wife, however, unhappy as she was with her husband's behavior, viewed the episodes as part of her lot in life as a woman. The husband viewed his own behavior as acceptable and, according to the wife, would brag about his behavior at social and family gatherings.

As with other forms of sexual abuse, the dynamics of spousal rape seem to have less relationship to sexual desire than to destructive patterns of conflict resolution and seem to be linked primarily to control issues in the marriage. Often the rape occurs during a separation or subsequent to the filing for divorce. For some husbands, rape of their spouse is equivalent to hitting or striking the spouse as a means of communicating their power in the relationship. Goode (1971) maintains that men who resort to violence in arguments with their wives may do so out of frustration with losing a "war of words" to a more verbally adept wife. He suggests that some marriages lack alternative means for bringing conflict to an end and "crushing the other can become a more tempting resolution to the interaction than any alternative" (p. 633). Sexual abuse of the spouse is that crushing of the other spouse in some marriages. As a particular form of spouse abuse, spouse sexual abuse often elicits less sympathy from others than spouse abuse without sexual acts. Not only is the wife often still regarded as the sexual property of her husband by many, but aggression and violence in the marriage, within certain limits, are still tolerated by many as acceptable, if not desirable. Boskey (1978) comments that "in many cases the fact that there is violence between the spouses in a marriage may be, for that couple, an appropriate means of dealing with the strains of daily living" (p. 203).

Sexual abuse by a spouse sometimes occurs in connection with the sexual abuse of children in the family. In such situations the perpetrator is most frequently a controlling father who not only abuses the children but also forces his wife to engage in sexual activities with the children while he watches. The pathology tends to be severe in such families. The father generally feels little if any remorse for his behavior and has little interest or motivation for changing his behavior. A therapist may become involved with the family in the aftermath of a report made to authorities or learn of the abuse in the course of treatment for another problem. Unfortunately, sometimes professionals have such difficulty accepting the possibility that those situations occur that they attribute the information revealed to a delusional system or other individual symptomatology and deny the reality of the information. For example:

> A 37-year-old married mother of 13 was admitted to a psychiatric unit after a suicide attempt. She complained of being forced by her husband to engage in intercourse and oral sex with her 14-year-old son. She further related that her husband forced the children, male and female, to have sex with him and with each other. For several months mental health professionals labeled her as psychotic and attributed the accounts of sexual abuse as part of the psychotic symptomatology. The therapist responsible for work with the family reported the abuse to the local child protective service agency. Even after the report was made, those investigating the report were dubious about the validity of the bizarre report since the father and children continued to deny the accusations and talked about the mother's "craziness." Finally, one of the children acknowledged that the mother was telling the truth and asked for protection from the father.

Abuse by Male Family Members Other Than Spouses

While reports of adult men being sexually abused by family members are rare to nonexistent, adult women do report sexual abuse by male family members other than spouses. Some reports involve a continuation of sexual abuse by fathers, brothers, or uncles that began in childhood or adolescence. Some women report sexual abuse by adolescent or adult sons.

> A middle-aged women was seen in crisis after seeking shelter in a domestic violence program. She left her farm home after her 22-year-old son raped her. She was chemically dependent and provided a history of physical abuse by her husband over the entire course of their 25-year marriage. A 17-year-old daughter left home several months before the mother's departure after telling her mother that her brother had attempted to rape her but that she had been able to flee. The woman was particularly distressed by the reaction of her husband, who laughed and accused his wife of seducing the son.

Alcohol and Drugs

Alcohol or other chemicals frequently play some role in intrafamily sexual abuse as in other types of domestic violence. Even when chemical dependency coexists with sexual abuse in a family, however, a direct causal relationship cannot be assumed. Victims in such families frequently report that the sexual abuse occurs both with and without concomitant use of chemicals. Treatment for each problem may need to be planned separately.

Child Abuse

Children who are sexually abused within their families form a distinct subgroup of abuse victims. On the basis of a retrospective survey of 796 undergraduate students from six New England colleges and universities, Finkelhor (1980) found that 19% of the women in his study had been sexually abused; 9% by a relative. Nine percent of the young men in the study reported sexual abuse during childhood, with the perpetrator likely to be a male person outside the family who was known to the child. An earlier study by DeFrancis (1969) of cases reported to law enforcement found that only 25% of the victims were abused by a stranger, whereas 37% were abused by friends or acquaintances of the family, 27% by a member of the household, and 11% by a relative. Subsequent analyses of sexual abuse reports have produced similar findings (Child Sexual Abuse Victim Assistance Project, 1978). In two decades, the estimates of the incidence of intrafamily child sexual abuse have increased 100-fold from 500 in 1955 (Weinberg, 1955) to 50,000 in 1976 (Giarretto, 1976).

Access to a child for sexual abuse appears most likely to occur through the family network of relatives, friends, and acquaintances. Although popular opinion might envision the typical victim to be an adolescent nymphet, abuse reports include children of all ages from infancy through adolescence. Although father-daughter abuse is most prevalent statistically, brother-sister and mother-son sexual relationships are believed to be underreported. Clinical practice provides examples of all combinations of relationships between family members. The abuse may entail an exclusive relationship between two family members or there may be multiple sexual relationships in the family.

If the problem of children sexually abused within their families were not so serious, the contradictions and misleading stereotypes regarding the dynamics in sexually abusive families might be amusing. In addition, most of the research on intrafamily child sexual abuse is conducted and analyzed without consideration or understanding of the family as a system. Therefore, demographics and individual pathologies are assessed, albeit with contradictory findings, but the richness of the interactive process within the family is overlooked by many researchers. Even in his analysis of the findings from the Child Sexual Abuse Treatment Program (CSATP), a pioneering model for family-focused treatment of intrafamily child sexual abuse developed by Henry Giarretto, Kroth (1979) was unable to provide more than superficial information about the structure and functioning of the sexually abusive families in that study. His findings are neither surprising nor particularly enlightening: 38% of the parents report that they have been arguing "quite a lot," 47% report deteriorating marital relationships, and 80% report nonexistent or declining sexual contacts with each other in the 2 months before entry into the program. The study finds the treatment effective in decreasing negative family as well as individual symptoms by comparing responses to questions at the beginning of treatment and near termination in several areas: a decrease from 47% to 6% ($p<.05$) in the number of couples reporting deteriorating relationships in the prior 2 months; a decrease from 57% to 0% ($p<.05$) undecided or contemplating a divorce or separation (although some of the original 57% were not included in the near-termination response because separation or divorce already had occurred); an increase from 5% to 59% of couples reporting improved relationships; an increase from 0% to 41% reporting increased sexual activity in the prior 2 months; and an increase from 0% to 50% ($p<.05$) of nonoffending spouses reporting experiencing orgasm quite a bit or a great deal.

Other analyses of family dynamics or characteristics focus almost exclusively on father-daughter abuse: an autocratic father who is ineffectual, has low self-esteem, and relates poorly to adults outside the family system; an unhealthy marriage with strained or nonexistent husband-wife sexual relationships; absence of one parent for periods of time because of illness, work schedule, etc.; overcrowding and lack of privacy; socioemotional or geographic isolation of the family; alcoholism; presence of a passive parent (usually mother) in the home; cultural and multigenerational patterns; and occurrence of a precipitating crisis, such as loss of a job. It is beyond the bounds of this article to critique the studies or quasi-studies that have contributed those descriptions to the literature. Note, however, that those findings and the findings of other studies purporting to describe the "typical" sexually abusive family should be viewed with a questioning, if not a skeptical mind. While some of those descriptions occur with enough frequency to make them useful in triggering awareness of "at risk" families, there are in fact no accurate stereotypes of sexually abusive families, except for the common linkages of pathological functioning in the marital relationship.

In view of the dearth of completed research on the dynamics of sexually abusive families, clinical observations can be helpful, but should be open to continued reevaluation and scrutiny. Clinical experience suggests that sexually abusive families fall within either the enmeshed or disengaged-chaotic categories. Perpetrators in some enmeshed families turn to children in the family when their marriages deteriorate instead of seeking sexual/emotional relationships outside the families. Perpetrators in enmeshed families often verbalize caring, loving feelings toward the victims. In contrast, perpetrators in disengaged-chaotic families are more likely to become involved in indiscriminate sexual relationships with family and nonfamily members and may use more brutality in their abuse. Few perpetrators can be diagnosed as pedophiles.

The phenomenon of destructive triangulation appears to be a principal feature of sexually abusive families. In a sophisticated and provocative discussion of related themes in the literature, Rist (1979) describes a three-generational model based on the dual dynamics of rejection and abandonment that culminates in an incestuous father-daughter relationship. As a consequence of the abuse, the child victim frequently learns to equate sexuality with affection and that seductive and sexual behaviors are rewarded with approval and even material gain or special privileges.

Discussion of the dynamics of sexually abusive families would be incomplete without reference to the role of the much maligned wife/mother in cases of father-daughter abuse. Some theorists clearly see the mother as the real culprit. Rosenfeld (1979) describes the mother as "likely to be a needful woman, insecure in her worth and femininity . . . [who] has frequently known about the incest . . ." (p. 407). Rist (1979) also describes the mother as a "dependent and infantile woman . . . [who] has given her daughter and husband covert but unambiguous messages . . . that the daughter is to assume the sexual functions normally exercised by the wife" (p. 687). While there are indeed some mothers who fit and thereby "prove" these descriptions, the family therapist should be wary of the tendency to single out the mother as blameful when the family system itself sets the stage for the sexual abuse and the responsibility for the sexual act belongs with the perpetrator. More recently, McIntyre (1981) has decried the scapegoating of mothers in sexually abusive families as sexist and nontherapeutic.

INTERVENTION BY THE FAMILY THERAPIST

It is important that the family therapist sort through the truths, half-truths, and overgeneralizations and fashion a therapeutic approach for the family with problems of sexual abuse. One of the many sets of variables that must be taken into account in developing that approach is the juncture at which the family therapist becomes involved. This discussion will use three time frames as organizational points for planning a therapeutic approach: point of discovery, post-discovery referral for treatment, and delayed treatment. The point of discovery is used because the decision "to tell" and obtain help usually is a more important indicator of the victim's and the family's readiness for treatment and change than the type of abuse or actual time lapse since the abuse occurred. In fact, intrafamily sexual abuse may continue over a period of many years before the point of discovery is reached.

Point of Discovery

The therapist may be the first person to suspect or learn that a family member has been sexually abused either by someone inside or outside the family system. In their 5-year follow-up of assault victims, Burgess and Holmstrom (1979) found that one-fourth of the adolescents and young adults in their sample did not tell any family members about the assault. Reasons for not telling included protection of family members from disturbing information, conflict of values, need to maintain independence, and emotional or geographic separation from family. Forty-two percent of the victims told selected family members and one-third told all family members. While there is no reason to believe that total disclosure by the victim to family is always the healthiest decision, the victim who does not or cannot turn to family for support may have greater difficulty recovering from the abusive experience, and the decision to avoid telling the family may be indicative of poor relationship patterns. For instance, if a married victim has not told her husband about an incident of sexual abuse, the therapist certainly would question the rules or expectations of the relationship.

The victim who seeks out a therapist as the first person to tell about a sexually abusive incident may do so immediately after the incident, while in the throes of the crisis, or after years of secrecy. If the victim is still in crisis, a crisis intervention approach, which would include some attention to practical issues and problem solving, would be indicated. The therapist should explore with the victim the possibility of disclosing the fact of the abuse to family members. Disclosure of the abuse could be arranged to take place during a family session with the therapist present. The victim and the family can prepare for the disclosure by discussing possible family reactions, which may include a broad spectrum of emotional and behavioral responses, such as anger or rage at the perpetrator, anger at the victim, guilt, denial, or overprotectiveness. The victim and the family will need to make decisions regarding the possibility of contacting law enforcement agencies and filing charges. The therapist should encourage a medical exam to rule out physical trauma and venereal disease.

When the abuse is revealed after a time lag, the therapist can assess the residual effects of the incident and begin the task of reconstructive work with the victim and the family if there is indication that the victim has not achieved resolution of the earlier abuse. The person's initial decision not to tell family members should be explored, and the decision should be reconsidered.

If the sexual abuse is a quasi-secret about two family members, the discovery of the abuse by the therapist is particularly volatile. An initial decision regarding telling of family members is made by the victim at the time of the assault or shortly thereafter.

> One 17-year-old girl ran next door to tell her grandmother within seconds of her stepfather's aborted attempt to fondle her genitals. The grandmother notified the mother who was at work and the family sought help from a therapist.
>
> In contrast, a 16-year-old girl who had been sexually abused by her stepfather at age 7 was sexually abused by a second stepfather at age 12. The family was in therapy at the time of the abuse, but the abuse was not revealed by the girl to the therapist or other family members. A brother discovered the abuse and told the mother, who notified the police. The stepfather was prosecuted and placed on probation under the condition that he receive therapy. The family reunited and contacted a different therapist, who also utilized a family therapy approach. After a year of therapy, sessions were decreased to an infrequent basis. A 13-year-old sister ran away from home at that point and, when she was found, asked to see the therapist. She revealed to the therapist that the father had resumed sexual activity with the 16-year-old sister and that her running away was a reaction to the father's approaching her also.

In the latter case, not only did family therapy not prevent the recurrence of the abuse, but the members who were victimized did not use the therapeutic setting or relationship to seek protection from the victimization. Family therapists frequently are dismayed to learn that a family seen in treatment was sexually abusive during the course of treatment; and adults abused as children frequently report being in therapy during the abuse but being too embarrassed or frightened to reveal the abuse to the therapist. The adults often recall wishing that their therapists would ask the right questions that would enable them to reveal their secret without guilt about betrayal of a family member.

Family therapists are not equipped with mind-reading equipment, but alertness to risk factors and signals of sexual abuse in families, along with the use of direct questions, reduces the possibility of blindness to intrafamily sexual abuse.

> A family was referred by a juvenile court for therapy because of the truancy and runaway behavior of a 14-year-old girl. The therapist saw the family consisting of both parents, the 14-year-old girl, and her 9-year-old brother. The marital relationship was reported as unsatisfactory by both parents. The mother had a chronic physical illness that confined her to bed with some pain for several days at a time. The mother appeared to be disengaged from the family interaction. When the therapist met with the marital couple alone, she commented that the mother's illness must make sharing a bed somewhat difficult. The father stated that he slept with his daughter to avoid making his wife uncomfortable. The therapist asked the father about sexual activity with the daughter. He denied any abuse. The 14-year-old, when initially questioned, denied the abuse. However, the therapist brought up the sleeping relationship in a later session and the girl confided that the father fondled her and had her masturbate him when he was in bed with her.

Some therapists are reluctant to use a direct approach to inquire about suspected intrafamily sexual abuse. In general, that reluctance can be attributed more to projection on the part of the therapist than to a valid rationale for avoidance of the subject. It is preferable to introduce the issue in individual sessions with the suspected victim, perpetrator, or other nonabusing family member than with the entire family unit present. The therapist can approach the topic with some discussion of generational boundaries and appropriate kinds of parent-child touching before asking directly about a sexual relationship. The therapist also should proceed with awareness that if family rules do not include prohibition of sexual activity among members, several sexual relationships may occur simultaneously or sequentially.

Nonverbal cues are extremely important in providing guidance to the therapist. Avoidance of eye contact, long pauses, or signs of anxiety may indicate the family member's dilemma in trying to decide how to respond. The therapist should proceed gently but firmly in pursuing the issue. Although many families deny the abuse when the question is first introduced, the opening of the issue by the therapist can result in desensitization of the family to the subject and lead to eventual willingness of a member to challenge the family rule that the abuse be kept secret. Frequently, a child will disclose the abuse, which is then denied by other family members. The child may then reconsider and deny that the abuse occurred with the explanation that he or she was lying or must have dreamed it. While there are rare situations in which children unjustly accuse family members of approaching them sexually, reports of sexual abuse by a child tend to be valid. In fact, subsequent retractions of the report by a child should be viewed with suspicion, because the retraction is often a product of a resurgence of the child's feelings of family loyalty and of pressure by the family system. When a child's accusation of sexual abuse is denied by the family, the therapist can refrain from assuming an investigative role and emphasize that the child's accusation represents problems in the family regardless of the accuracy of the report or family differences of opinion about what happened.

Reporting Abuse

If sexual abuse is uncovered, family therapists are ethically, and often legally, bound to report the abuse to the appropriate authorities. There are statutes in each state requiring the reporting of child sexual abuse as a form of child abuse, and those statutes specifically negate the use of confidentiality or privileged communication as a reason for not reporting. The statutes generally provide immunity from civil suit for the person reporting. Typically, the language of the laws does not require that a person reporting have absolute knowledge or proof that the abuse occurred, only that there is reason to suspect that the abuse has occurred.

The reporting of child sexual abuse can be a controversial issue among family therapists. Arguments against reporting include (1) allegiance to the principle of absolute confidentiality as a higher priority than legal requirements or protection of the child and (2) belief that the sexual abuse can be treated more effectively by the therapist without the intervention of agencies responsible for investigating and managing cases of child sexual abuse. Many therapists express concern that the family will leave treatment if the abuse is reported. While those arguments are not without substance, they do reflect a somewhat grandiose attitude, which cannot be justified pragmatically in actual clinical experience.

The family will not necessarily withdraw from treatment with the therapist who makes the report. Moreover, if treatment with the reporting therapist is abandoned, the family often is required to resume therapy by the court or a child protective service agency.

The primary arguments for reporting are the legal requirement to report and the therapist's ethical obligation to protect the vulnerable child in the family. Although the family system may be opened to treatment by the revelation of the "family secret," the system will begin its self-righting tendencies to reestablish equilibrium and will often return to former patterns of sexual abuse within a year unless treatment is effective. Because of risks of recidivism or precipitous or untimely withdrawal from treatment, Giarretto, Giarretto, and Sgroi (1978) strongly advocate use of an agent such as the court, which represents authority, to provide needed leverage to motivate families to stay in treatment and work toward treatment goals.

Post-Discovery Referral for Treatment

When individuals or families seek treatment to deal with the effects of sexual abuse, the distinction between abuse by a family member and abuse by a nonfamily member is a critical determinant of therapeutic approach. The issue of divided loyalty generally makes treatment of intrafamily abuse more complex. Some abuse situations where the perpetrator is a family friend constitute a gray area between the categories of intrafamily abuse and extrafamily abuse. In those situations family members also may experience divided loyalty.

> A 12-year-old girl was forced by her aunt's boyfriend to have intercourse. The assault occurred in the girl's home during a visit by the aunt and the boyfriend while other family members were away. The aunt was drunk and sleeping in a bedroom. She did not respond to the girl's cries for help even when she left the bedroom to answer the telephone. The girl told her mother, who confronted the aunt and the boyfriend. The boyfriend did not deny the fact that intercourse occurred, but maintained that the girl seduced him. The aunt, who was the mother's sister and for whom the girl had been named, sided with her boyfriend. The mother supported her daughter and severed her ties with her sister. Treatment of the adjustment to the rape was complicated by the mother's and daughter's feelings of abandonment and loss of a close family member.

The victim abused by someone outside the family is fortunate if the family has a previous history of positive coping with crisis and stress and can provide a positive environment of mutual support. In such a case, the role of the therapist may be limited to crisis intervention and encouragement of the family's previously developed self-righting tendencies. As with other crises, sexual abuse may cause temporary disruption and negative symptoms for the healthy family. Those qualities that will allow the family to handle the stress and reestablish a healthy level of functioning are familiar to family therapists: a repertoire of positive response mechanisms character-ized by depth and flexibility; predictable and stable role expectations; respect and acceptance of individual differences; clear, direct, open, and consistent communication patterns; a realistic distinction between what family members can expect from one another and what each must provide for themselves; and a sense of trust that family members will receive something of value from the family approximately equal to what is contri-buted to the family.

Families requiring more intensive work will be those with a history of unresolved issues and problems. In such families, there is a risk that the crisis surrounding the abuse will be used to intensify or accelerate preexist-ing conflicts. The sexual abuse may be just one of many problems for which the family has sought treatment or it may be the "straw that breaks the camel's back" and propels a family with previously unidentified problems into treatment. Holmstrom and Burgess (1979) recognize the role of the abusive event in the life of the family as follows: "By precipitating a crisis, rape illuminates certain attitudes and role expectations in a dramatic way, thus making them more visible than they are in the routine of everyday life" (p. 329). Unfortunately, most rape crisis programs are oriented to work with the victim on a short-term basis and may overlook the need for family intervention and long-term counseling (King & Webb, 1981).

An important variable for the therapist to consider is the family's interpre-tation of the meaning of the abuse, whether it is viewed primarily as an act of violence or an act of sexuality (Holmstrom & Burgess, 1979; White & Rollins, 1981). Since the victim experiences the abuse as an act of violence, a family definition of the event as sexual can confuse and frustrate the victim. The therapist's role will be to clarify the meaning of the abuse and help the family arrive at a shared definition of the experience. Cultural factors must be considered in working with the family since many traditional cultures view any participation in sex, voluntary or involuntary, by a woman outside a marriage relationship as defiling the woman.

Husbands and other male family members may exhibit responses arising out of the societal expectation that men protect women. With the historical view of women as property, rape has been viewed as an insult to the man, father or husband, who "owned" the woman (Brownmiller, 1975). Some vestige of that viewpoint remains in many families today (Silverman, 1978). The issue of guilt over failure to protect a family member is often a crit-ical factor in situations in which the victim is a child. White and Rollins (1981) stress the importance of assisting the family in externalizing the blame for the abuse as an important step toward positive post-abuse reorganization.

Although the majority of husbands or other family members react to sexual abuse of a member by someone outside the family with anger and blaming of the perpetrator, there are some husbands or other family members who will blame the victim (Holmstrom & Burgess, 1979; Miller, Williams & Bernstein, 1982; Williams, 1981). The blaming of the victim usually is associated with a viewpoint that the abuse is a sexual rather than a violent act.

Post-rape sexual relationships often are negatively affected by the rape (Kilpatrick et al., 1981; McCahill et al., 1979; Miller et al., 1982). Therapists may utilize various approaches to work toward improvement of the sexual relationship. An initial step would be review of the couples' preabuse sexual relationship. If the preabuse sexual relationship was unsatisfying for either or both partners, the abuse may provide a convenient rationale for avoiding sex and there may be little initial motivation to deal with the sexual consequences to the couple relationship.

For all couples, timing of the resumption of intercourse will depend on the nature and degree of physical trauma to the victim. After the victim has recovered physically, the aversive experience of the abuse may contaminate the sexual relationship with the spouse or other sexual partner. Attention to communication is a key element in treatment of any sexual dysfunction resulting from sexual abuse, as it is in the treatment of sexual dysfunction in general. Avoidance of communication about the abuse and the feelings engendered by the abuse is common (Miller et al., 1982). The task of the therapist will be to encourage both partners to give permission to each other to talk about the abuse and its emotional aftermath. Since the emotional sequelae may include phobic responses, a behavioral approach such as systematic desensitization may be helpful.

In cases of intrafamily sexual abuse, the therapist must abandon the notion that he or she may be intervening with a healthy family. Sexually abusive families are by definition dysfunctional when the abuse is viewed as a symptom of family dysfunction. A family that has been identified as sexually abusive usually will be involved with other systems outside the family in addition to therapy, such as juvenile or family court, criminal court, child protective services, and foster care systems. The family therapist is usually the person most capable of understanding and interpreting the sexual abuse as a family problem and may need to be an advocate to encourage other systems impinging on the family to assess potential interventions in terms of their possible ramifications within the family system.

When intrafamily child sexual abuse is uncovered, there is the risk of disintegration of the family unit, which is often more fearful for the victim than the actual abuse. By the time the family reaches the therapist, one or more family members may be living outside the family home. Working from the belief that the child has a right to be protected from further abuse, several options for living arrangements are possible: family remaining together with therapy and supervision by a child protective agency; temporary removal of the abuser from the family with the goal of eventually reuniting the family; removal of the abused child to an out-of-home placement with the goal of eventually reuniting the family; and separation of the family with no plans to reunite the family. It is important that the family therapist have a role in those decisions, which are often imposed on the family by the outside systems. Certainly, the therapeutic plan will vary with the decisions made about living arrangements, but it is important to use a family approach in treatment even when family members are living apart.

Because the family often is subject to decisions regarding living arrangements that are imposed by others, thereby removing control regarding those decisions from the family, a major task of the therapist is to assist the family in settling down and starting to work on family problems, rather than expending all their energy on battles with outside agencies.

Although the treatment approach for each sexually abusive family must be determined after thorough assessment, as with treatment of any other family, it is possible to anticipate some common problems and themes and make general suggestions. Therapy with a family focus can proceed through sessions with the family as a unit; sessions with individuals; and sessions with targeted subsystems, such as parental subsystems, the sibling subsystems, the mother-daughter dyad, and the father-daughter dyad. The subsystem categories might be adjusted for the types of abuse other than father-daughter. General issues and tasks in sexually abusive families may include individuation; definition of generational boundaries; softening of boundaries between an isolated family and the surrounding community; examination and renegotiation of family rules regarding affection, touching and sexuality; examination and renegotiation of role expectations; and exploration of relationships in the parents' family of origin. Since chemical dependency often coexists in a family with sexual abuse, a chemical dependency assessment should be routine, with referral to specialized chemical dependency resources if necessary.

Family therapists should align themselves firmly with the incest taboo to create appropriate prohibitions that may not have been learned by the parents in their own families of origin. The abuser and the family may collude in defending the intrafamily sexual relationship with a variety of sometimes very creative rationalizations: "He [or she] seduced me." (This explanation does not depend on the age of the victim and has been used to justify sex with a preschool child.) "She was sleeping around and I thought it was better to keep it in the family." "I was just trying to prepare her for what it would be like when she got married." "I was just checking to see if her bed (or pants) were wet." "I couldn't be unfaithful to my wife" (by having sex with someone outside the family). "I was drunk and didn't realize what I was doing." "I love her like a girlfriend, not like a daughter." The therapist must take the position that the abuser is responsible for his or her own sexual behavior and as an adult is responsible for protection of the child, who lacks both the ability to give informed consent for sex and the power to refuse to have sex with the adult who is in an authority position (Finkelhor, 1979). The therapist can work with the family to redefine the meaning of the sexual activity from a need for sexual gratification to a need for control, an attempt to alleviate feelings of low self-worth, or whatever nonsexual meanings the therapist perceives.

In addition to issues that the family needs to address as a unit, individuals and subsystems may have separate issues. It is extremely important to recognize and deal with the pain of all family members. Unfortunately, nonabused siblings frequently are overlooked in the treatment process although they also are affected by the abuse (Kroth, 1979). Siblings should be included in the treatment.

Once the abuse is uncovered, the child often is victimized again, by the response of family members who blame the victim for the disruption of family life and by professionals who are insensitive to their feelings. The children, often believing that their participation in the sexual activity was necessary to preserve the family, may feel guilt surrounding a number of issues, such as the belief that they were responsible for the abuse; possible feelings of pleasure, including orgasm, experienced during the sexual activity; special privileges gained from cooperating with the abuser; a sense of responsibility for breaking up the family or sending the abuser to jail; or a competitive relationship with the nonabusing parent. Various approaches can be used to address those issues. Abusers can be encouraged to take a leadership role by giving the family the clear message that they were responsible for the sexual activity. Restructuring of the system to reduce the child's sense of omnipotence is important, as is redirection and redefinition of the anger toward the child. Individual sessions to work with the child on possible ambivalent feelings toward the parent and the pleasurable responses to the sexual activity are often necessary.

By the time the family reaches therapy, the child-victim frequently has developed self-defeating and manipulative behaviors. Because the pattern of sexual abuse is embedded in a dysfunctional family system, it is not really possible to attribute the totality of the victim's problems to the sexual abuse. Usually the victim cooperates with and demonstrates loyalty to the family by moving from the victim role to the scapegoat role. If he or she engages in chemical abuse, truancy, defiance, promiscuity, or running away, the family can self-righteously say, "I told you so." The therapist's reframing of the self-destructive behaviors makes it more difficult for the victim and the family to maintain their destructive roles and expectations.

Working with the marital dyad requires attention to renegotiation of co-parenting roles and development of more positive parenting approaches. The couple's sexual relationship is invariably poor. The nonabusing parent may need to work toward desensitization of aversive responses if the thought of a sexual relationship triggers visions of the abuser and the victim engaged in sexual activity. In many cases, neither spouse has ever enjoyed a satisfactory sexual relationship and work on sexual issues must proceed in a very basic way.

The dyadic relationships between the victim and each parent need special attention. In cases of father-daughter abuse, there are several potential mother-daughter issues to be resolved: the daughter's anger at her mother for failing to protect her, the competitive mother-daughter relationship, mother-daughter role reversal, and mutual feelings of betrayal and guilt. If families plan to stay together but deny the competitive elements of the mother-daughter relationship, the therapist may pose the question: "How would you feel if Mr. X were sleeping with the woman down the street and she came to dinner?" The daughter initially may feel vulnerable if the mother decides to stay with her husband and work on the marriage. There is a sense of double rejection and displacement; her parents have chosen each other over her. However, the identification of feelings of vulnerability can provide a transition point in the movement and restructuring of family patterns.

Child-victims may refuse to attend a session with the abuser. The initial goal adopted by the therapist is to prepare both for an eventual meeting in a therapeutic session during which they must begin to address unresolved feelings for each other and renegotiate their relationship. In that session, the abuser must acknowledge his responsibility for the abuse and make a commitment that it will not be repeated (Giarretto, 1976). Some abusers are not readily available for family therapy because of separation or divorce of the parents. Although techniques such as role playing, double chairing, or writing a letter can be used, a face-to-face session between victim and abuser is most effective.

Delayed Treatment

Therapy may be initiated after an interval of several or many years. The delayed response may be related to a past incident of abuse by someone within or outside the family. There is usually a triggering event and the individual may be encouraged by a spouse to enter treatment. The victim may have believed that the earlier event was buried and thereby resolved, only to experience a resurgence of the unresolved issues. Symptoms may vary and include sexual dysfunction, sexual identity conflicts, depression, self-destructive behaviors, physical complaints, and phobias. The tasks in therapy are similar to those outlined for treatment that takes place closer to the event, but resolution is complicated by the fact that the victim usually has developed some nonadaptive mechanisms for handling feelings about the abuse and those mechanisms have become rigid over time. If the abuse was by a family member, the abuser may be dead or unavailable to become part of the treatment process. It is not uncommon for an individual to begin therapy with rather vague memories of a sexually abusive home and have gross deficits in remote memory of certain phases of his or her childhood. Hypnosis is an option that could be explored as part of the treatment plan in such cases. If memories of the abuse are available, they should be drawn upon to reconstruct the abusive incident in relation to other important aspects of the individual's life, particularly family relationships, at that time. A focus on getting in touch with memories of family relationships at the time of the abuse connects with examination of the individual's current family patterns. With awareness of how past and current family patterns work to prevent resolution of the earlier abuse, the therapist can plan appropriate interventions.

Occasionally there will be a connection between the points of entry into therapy that bring the family through a full circle.

A 20-year-old woman sought treatment to resolve problems resulting from sexual abuse by her stepfather that occurred between the ages of 12 and 16. Two sisters and a brother were also abused by the stepfather, who forced them to have sex with each other. The mother was aware of the abuse but took no steps to protect the children. The entry into treatment was precipitated by complaints from the young woman's boyfriend that she was "cold" and "a tease." During the first session the therapist explored the woman's current relationships and discovered that two younger half-brothers, ages 12 and 14, were still in the home. The therapist assisted the young woman in contacting the child protection agency, which investigated and found that the 14-year-old boy was being sexually abused by the father. Therapy proceeded using a combination of formats with various groupings present at sessions. The woman who initially entered treatment sought out her biological father and reestablished contact with him, in addition to achieving some of her other goals. The parents and the two sons were reunited after short-term foster care placement for the boys and the family achieved some necessary changes through treatment. By asking the right questions and responding actively to the individual's portrayal of the family unit, the therapist was able not only to assist the young woman to make desired changes, but also to initiate dramatic changes in the dysfunctional family of origin.

SUMMARY

Family therapy has been underutilized as an intervention in cases of sexual abuse, although sexual abuse of a member clearly has implications for the family system and the response of the family has implications for the victim. Since both the awareness of the problem of sexual abuse and the number of sexual abuse cases have increased, family therapists can expect to see sexually abused individuals in their practice. Family therapists need to be knowledgeable about the emotional sequelae of sexual abuse for the victim and the family in order to provide effective treatment. Therapy with the victim and the family should take into account distinctions between abuse by a family member and abuse by a nonfamily member, distinctions between abuse of a child and abuse of an adult, and the point of entry into treatment. Much has been discovered and learned about sexual abuse within recent years, and family therapists will be in the vanguard of refining and further developing the current state of knowledge.

REFERENCES

Boskey, J.B. Spousal abuse in the United States: The attorney's role. In J.M. Eckelear & S.N. Katz (Eds.), *Family violence: An international and interdisciplinary study*. Toronto: Butterworths, 1978.

Brownmiller, S. *Against our will: Men, women and rape*. New York: Simon & Schuster, 1975.

Burgess, A.W., & Holmstrom, L.L. *Rape: Victims of crisis*. Bowie, Md.: Robert J. Brady, Co., 1974.

Burgess, A.W., & Holmstrom, L.L. *Rape: Crisis and recovery*. Bowie, Md.: Robert J. Brady Co., 1979.

Caplan, G. *Principles of preventive psychiatry*. New York: Basic, 1964.

Child Sexual Abuse Victim Assistance Project: Year Two Proposal. Washington, D.C.: Law Enforcement Assistance Administration, U.S. Department of Justice, Children's Hospital National Medical Center, 1978.

DeFrancis, V. *Protecting the child victim of sex crimes*. Denver: American Humane Association, 1969.

Finkelhor, D. What's wrong with sex between adults and children? Ethics and the problem of sexual abuse. *American Journal of Orthopsychiatry*, 1979, *49*(4), 692-697.

Finkelhor, D. Risk factors in the sexual victimization of children. *Child Abuse and Neglect*, 1980, *464*, 265-273.

Fox, S.S., & Scherl, D.J. Crisis intervention with victims of rape. *Social Work*, 1972, *17*(1), 37-42.

Giarretto, H. Humanistic treatment of father-daughter incest. In R.E. Helfer & G.H. Kempe (Eds.), *Child abuse and neglect: The family and the community*. Cambridge, Mass.: Ballinger, 1976.

Giarretto, H., Giarretto, A., & Sgroi, S.M. Coordinated community treatment of incest. In A.W. Burgess, A.N. Groth, L.L. Holmstrom, & S.M. Sgroi (Eds.), *Sexual assault of children and adolescents*. Lexington, Mass.: Lexington Books, 1978.

Goode, W.J. Force and violence in the family. *Journal of Marriage and the Family*, 1971, *33*(1), 624-636.

Green, K.J. An overview of major contributions to family therapy. In R.J. Green & R.L. Framo (Eds.), *Family therapy: Major contributions*. New York: International Universities Press, 1981.

Holmstrom, L.L., & Burgess, A.W. Rape: The husband's and boyfriend's initial reactions. *The Family Coordinator*, 1979, *28*, 321-330.

Kilpatrick, D.G., Resick, P.A., & Veronen, L.J. Effects of a rape experience: A longitudinal study. *Journal of Social Issues*, 1981, *37*(4), 105-122.

King, H.E., & Webb, C. Rape crisis centers: Progress and problems. *Journal of Social Issues*, 1981, *37*(4), 93-104.

Kroth, J.A. *Child sexual abuse: Analysis of a family therapy approach*. Springfield, Ill.: Charles C Thomas, 1979.

McCahill, T.W., Meyer, L.C., & Fishman, A.M. *The aftermath of rape*. Lexington, Mass.: Lexington Books, 1979.

McIntyre, K. Role of mothers in father-daughter incest: A feminist analysis. *Social Work*, 1981, *26*(6), 462-466.

Miller, W.R., Williams, A.M., & Bernstein, M.H. The effects of rape on marital and sexual adjustment. *American Journal of Family Therapy*, 1982, *10*(1), 51-58.

Rist, K. Incest: Theoretical and clinical views. *American Journal of Orthopsychiatry*, 1979, *49*(4), 680-691.

Rosenfeld, A.A. Endogamic incest and the victim-perpetrator model. *American Journal of Diseases of Children*, 1979, *133*, 406-410.

Silverman, D.O. Sharing the crisis of rape: Counseling the mates and families of victims. *American Journal of Orthopsychiatry*, 1978, *30*(1), 103-109.

Weinberg, S.K. *Incest behavior*. New York: Citadel Press, 1955.

White, P.M., & Rollins, C.R. Rape: A family crisis. *Family Relations*, 1981, *30*(1), 103-109.

Williams, A.S. Couple counseling with rape victims. In A.S. Gurman, (Ed.), *Questions and answers in family therapy*. New York: Brunner/Mazel, 1981.

7. Sexuality and Disability

Thomas Ward-McKinlay, PhD
Clinical Psychologist
Spinal Injury Unit
Casa Colina Hospital
Pomona, California

Julie G. Botvin-Madorsky, MD
Director
Spinal Injury Unit
Casa Colina Hospital
Pomona, California

Clinical Assistant Professor of
  Rehabilitation Medicine
University of California at Irvine

Assistant Clinical Professor of Psychiatry
  and Biobehavioral Sciences
University of California at Los Angeles

Candace Ward-McKinlay, PhD
Clinical Psychologist
Brain Injury Unit
Casa Colina Hospital
Pomona, California

In DISCUSSING THE ISSUE OF SEXUALITY AND THE DISABLED person, it is extremely important to define precisely what the term "sexuality" means. Trieschman (1980) emphasizes the importance of differentiating "sex drive," "sex acts," and "sexuality" when dealing with an individual who has a physical disability.

Sex, as a drive, is similar to other primary drives, including hunger and thirst. An individual's sex drive is affected by a complex set of interrelationships among various body systems and the external environment. It is assumed that under normal developmental circumstances and environmental conditions the sex drive will flourish and function appropriately. But what happens when a disability enters the picture? Does the sex drive diminish or disappear? Trieschman (1980) responds that, at least with spinal injured individuals, the sex drive remains, and should be a focus of comprehensive rehabilitation, just like other aspects of human functioning. Similarly, sexual interest is often maintained in such conditions as cerebrovascular accident, multiple sclerosis, cerebral palsy, and muscular dystrophy.

Sex acts, of course, are the actual behaviors engaged in during a sexual encounter. They generally involve the erogenous zones, but may not necessarily include intercourse. Sexual behavior is an extension of the sex drive. The issue addressed here is what happens when certain activities formerly engaged in for sexual pleasure are no longer possible or desirable because of disability? Does the individual become less sexual? The responses to these questions must take into account the disabled individual's attitudes and feelings about the expression of sexual affection, especially if what is now physically available to the individual is viewed initially as unacceptable or alien. One can easily discern therapeutic challenges in this area.

Each person, able-bodied or otherwise, experiences his or her sexuality in a unique and idiosyncratic manner. Sexuality is a broad and dynamic concept that incorporates many facets of an individual's being. Berkman, Weissman, and Frielich (1978) define sexuality as a dynamic process based on developmental learning experiences and having three basic components. The first is the psychosexual component, which is characterized by the individual's self-concept. The second is a social sexual component, which involves relationships with others. The third is the behavioral aspect, which is characterized by specific sexual acts or behaviors. Sexual development is seen as an ongoing process that is subject to the influences of an individual's life experiences, needs, and physical liabilities.

It is in looking at sexuality from a broader perspective that therapists can truly begin to appreciate and understand the significant interpersonal dynamics surrounding it. Without this understanding, fast "cookbook" approaches may appear the best source for dealing with the sexual concerns of the disabled; in other words, it is much easier to define a problem and apply a stock solution than to encounter and struggle with the numerous types of sexual issues presented to us by the disabled. As Cole (1975) has so aptly pointed out, ''Sexuality, like other birthrights, cannot be taken away by society; society may channel sexual attitudes and expressions, but it cannot prohibit all the forms and transformations generated by sexual energy.'' Therapists interested in working with the disabled must be ready to accept the challenges inherent in helping clients with sexual issues.

DEALING WITH THE SEXUAL NEEDS OF THE DISABLED

Significant changes have taken place over the past ten years in three basic treatment-related areas. The first is the area of sexual information for the disabled. Until the early 1970s, there was little material available that was accurate, and acceptable to the disabled. One of the reasons for this was the belief of many health care providers that disabled people were somehow asexual. Perhaps many practitioners did not choose to address sexual issues because of their own discomfort in discussing sexual matters, the so-called ''sexual revolution'' of the late 1960s notwithstanding. Many well-intentioned practitioners, having made a prior judgment about the sexual potential of their disabled clients, may have bypassed the topic so as not to ''embarrass'' these individuals.

Fortunately, however, significant developments have taken place to increase the availability of accurate sexual information to the disabled. This has been due, in part, to the pioneering efforts of Cole (1975) and Hohmann (1972), and others who have advocated the dissemination of appropriate sex education material to the disabled. In addition, the overall cultural impetus of increased openness about sexuality has had its impact on disabled individuals. As a result, there are now numerous books, films, manuals, and professional publications dealing with this issue in varying degrees of explicitness. Multi-Media Publications, for example, is recognized as a primary source of sex education material for the disabled.

Another area that has undergone a significant transformation is that of professional training. Many training and information resource agencies devoted to the sexual needs of the disabled have come into existence. Bullard and Knight (1981) have compiled a comprehensive list of such agencies. The popularity of Sexual Attitude Reassessment (SAR) workshops described by Cole, Chilgren, and Rosenberg (1973) has also contributed significantly to the training of health professionals in sexuality and disability. The SAR process has been demonstrated to be effective not only in imparting factual information to participants, but more important, in allowing them to develop a better understanding of their own sexuality. This increased awareness of one's own sexual identity is crucial in the validation process involved in dealing with clients. How can therapists hope to help others define and explore their sexuality if they are unclear or unsure about their own. Training programs that enhance therapists' sensitivity to disabled clients' needs are increasingly in demand.

The third and possibly most important development in the area of sexuality and disability has been in the attitude and behavior of disabled persons themselves. As a result of their growing awareness and acceptance of themselves as a viable political and sociological force, the disabled have become more assertive with respect to their rights as individuals and as a group. Along with this increased militancy has come an openness to explore, discuss, and challenge various societal proscriptions regarding their sexuality. Bullard and Knight (1981) provide an excellent collection of personal perspectives about sexuality written by educators and disabled individuals that honestly and accurately represents a wide cross section of their practical concerns. Similarly, Corbet (1980), in a film entitled *Outside* and a book entitled *Options,* provides a forum for disabled individuals to express their views on a wide variety of issues as well as to share the reality of their lives. These efforts in relating to the able-bodied world are even more significant because they represent a recognition and even a celebration of self. Reading these accounts, one is struck by the reality of the problems as well as by the creativity with which individuals deal with them.

There is no pity or false admiration here, simply an affirmation that the disabled struggle to meet their needs as others do. The key point is that basically the needs are the same. People with various disabilities are breaking out of old, passive, dependent molds and aggressively seeking—even demanding—what is rightfully theirs. In looking back at the definition of sexuality, it is easy to draw parallels between the able-bodied and the disabled with regard to the issues of personal and sexual adjustment.

THE IMPACT OF DISABILITY ON SEXUALITY

In exploring the impact of physical disability upon an individual's sexual functioning, several basic concerns must, of necessity, be dealt with. The first involves the organic nature of the individual's disability. While it is apparent that some sexual issues may be common to many types of disability, it is important to determine which specific aspects of an individual's disability are likely to affect which aspects of his or her sexual functioning. Cole and Cole (1978) have pointed out that not all disabilities directly affect genital functioning and that sexuality must not be simply equated with genitality. Our sexuality is interrelated with our manner of presenting ourselves to others. Such elements as body shape, activities, relationships, proclivities, and aversions are all part of the totality. Tables 7-1 through 7-4, adapted from Cole and Cole (1978), illustrate the relationship between type of disability and its effect on sexuality.

The primary feature of the types of disorders shown in Table 7-1 is time of onset. The knowledge that a child has a disability that will become more severe is likely to have far-ranging effects both upon the child and the family. Despite the fact that many progressive conditions do not affect sexual functioning directly, there is often a covert message to the child that sexual behavior may be too physically or emotionally demanding and should thus be ignored. Often parents and health care practitioners, believing that they are working in the child's best interest, effect a type of benign collusion in not dealing with the potential sexual needs of the child. Obviously, nothing could be less beneficial. The end result of such a conspiracy is an individual who may lack the necessary information and related confidence to establish intimate relationships.

Family members are often shocked to find that the patient does have sexual needs and is seeking ways to satisfy them. In these cases, the focus of

Table 7-1 Effects of Progressive Physical Disability on Sexuality When Time of Onset Is Before Puberty

	Masturbation	Coitus	Fertility	Appearance to Society
Diseases of Brain				M,F
Diseases of Spinal Cord	M,F	M	M	M,F
Musculoskeletal Diseases	M,F	M,F	M	M,F
Metabolic or Deficiency Diseases				M,F
Heart Disease				M,F
Blindness				M,F
Deafness				M,F

Note: M, male; F, female.

psychosocial intervention may be the family, rather than the child who is the identified patient. As the child grows, it is the family's responsibility to appropriately introduce information related to sexuality. The practitioner can assist this process by being aware of the deficits and resources of the family as a unit and by being available at crucial stress points in the development of the child as he or she faces the disability process. It is equally important to enable families to develop their own crisis coping systems.

The essential feature of the types of disabilities shown in Table 7-2 is the suddenness of occurrence. There is no time to prepare for the stresses that are involved in sudden onset of disability. Often a sense of crisis pervades the acute, reactive stage of adjustment, with the danger of depression and hopelessness following as realization of the permanent consequences sets in. Much will depend upon previous sexual and social experiences when determining appropriate areas for intervention. The greatest initial need may be for information, the assumption being that more therapy-related issues may surface later in the patient's adjustment process. The focus will obviously be on adjustment to the sequelae, both physical and psychological, to assist the patient in restructuring those areas of his or her life that are most affected. More directive counseling may be necessary because of the impact of disability upon masturbation, coitus, and fertility.

Table 7-2 Effects of Suddenly Acquired Physical Disability on Sexuality When Time of Onset Is After Puberty

	Masturbation	Coitus	Fertility	Appearance to Society
Spinal Cord Motor and Sensory Loss	M,F	M	M	M,F
Spinal Cord Motor Paralysis Only	M,F			M,F
Skeletal: Amputation or Deformity	M,F	M,F		M,F
External Genital	M,F	M,F	M	
Disfiguring Injuries				M,F
Enterostomy	M,F	M	M	
Blindness				M,F
Deafness				M,F

Note: M, male; F, female.

The essential feature of the disorders shown in Table 7-3 is that they are progressive. Much work will be needed to educate and prepare these patients and significant others for necessary adjustments. Again, there must be an emphasis on correct information regarding the course of disability so that patients and families can begin to work on adaptation to the process as it occurs. Support from family and significant others will be crucial in these disorders as functions gradually change or deteriorate. There is often a tendency for families to overreact and arrive at a pessimistic case assessment long before the specific issues of concern even arise.

The disorders shown in Table 7-4 are characterized by stable nonprogressive features. Among this group, only spinal injury has significant impact on masturbation, coitus, and fertility. Therapists dealing with persons having these disabilities should focus primarily on familial and psychosocial needs. Familial and parental information sharing is crucial here to ensure appropriate adjustment. This is similar to progressive disorders of childhood. The difference, of course, is the stable nature of the process. Adaptation can be maximized early as the child comes to accept the relative permanency of the disability. Other important factors to be considered center on familial assistance in allowing active exploration of sexual issues as a normal part of growth and development. Therapists may assist most in this aspect of the disability by reassuring families that patients need to try and sometimes fail in their attempts to adapt.

In reviewing the tables presented, it becomes readily apparent that many disorders affect sexuality only to the extent that the affected individual may

Table 7-3 Effects of Progressive Physical Disability on Sexuality When Time of Onset Is After Puberty

	Masturbation	Coitus	Fertility	Appearance to Society
Heart Disease		M,F		
Stroke				M,F
Diabetes Mellitus	M,F	M	M	
Muscular Dystrophy				M,F
Multiple Sclerosis	M,F	M	M	M,F
Skeletal: Amputation or Deformity	M,F	M,F		M,F
Renal Disease—End Stage	M,F	M	M	

Note: M, male; F, female.

Table 7-4 Effects of Stable Physical Disability on Sexuality When Time of Onset Is Before Puberty

	Masturbation	Coitus	Fertility	Appearance to Society
Brain Injury				M,F
Spinal Cord: Motor Sensory Loss	M,F	M	M	M,F
Altered Body Growth				M,F
Heart Disease				
Blindness				M,F
Deafness				M,F

Note: M, male; F, female.

appear different from others. Actual physical or genital functioning may not be grossly affected. This does not mean that the problems inherent in the situation are lessened, but rather that they must be dealt with in the appropriate intra- and interpersonal context in which they exist. It is important to emphasize this point, since many practitioners tend to force the disabled into a programmed sexual adjustment format that actually may not meet the patient's and his or her partner's true needs. The practitioner may work toward the goal of assisting a couple to become more genitally sexually active by suggesting a variety of adjusted positions, aids, and stimuli, while overlooking the individual's concerns about self-image or the couple's patterns of communication with respect to intimacy, whether physical or emotional.

Professional literature now exists that addresses the myriad concerns of persons with various disabilities. A brief review of this literature is presented before dealing with the practical clinical concerns of practitioners who work with members of this population.

SPINAL CORD INJURY (SCI)

Spinal cord injury has received much coverage in the clinical and research literature over the past few years, primarily because of the high visibility and militancy of SCI persons regarding sexual issues. Trieschman (1980) provides an excellent review of spinal injury in general, and sexuality in particular; relevant research in the areas of sex drive, sexual activities, neurophysiology, sexuality, and sex therapy is presented. Rabin (1980) presents similar data in a practical handbook form that is useful for the professional and lay person alike. Other works by Comarr and Vigue (1978) and Hohmann (1972) provide both technical and practical information on sex and spinal injury.

Factors That Influence Sexual Activity

In dealing with individuals who have spinal cord injuries, it is important to know the basic anatomical and neurophysiological features that are involved in sexual activity. From a strictly neurophysiological point of view, the male response cycle can be divided into four stages: erection, emission, ejaculation, and orgasm. This progression takes place in the able-bodied, but not necessarily for the individual with a spinal injury. The extent to which this cycle is disrupted depends on several factors. The first is degree of completeness of lesion. If the spinal cord is totally severed or destroyed at a certain point, this is termed a complete injury. All other lesions are called incomplete and obviously encompass a large "gray area" with regard to function. Another important factor is the location of the injury. Injuries at different levels of the spinal cord affect different aspects of the sexual response cycle. The spinal cord is divided into specific segments, which are numbered. These are the cervical (1-8); the thoracic (1-12); the lumbar (1-5); and the sacral (1-5). It is important to note that segments of the spinal cord do not coincide with the numbers of the vertebrae in the spinal column. This is because of the way in which the nerve roots leave the cord through the vertebrae. For simplicity's sake, reference in this discussion is to the cord segments and not to the vertebral units.

Injuries occurring at a specified level in the cord will influence those functions that are affected by the nerve segments that enter and exit the cord below the level of injury. Any activities that involve the brain may be affected (depending on degree of completeness), since the connections, in this case the nerves, have been injured; thus the impulses are disrupted. Other activities that do not require brain involvement, such as reflexes, may not be involved unless, of course, they are at the precise level at which the cord was injured. A simple example may elucidate the matter: an individual who has a complete lesion at T10 (the tenth thoracic segment of the cord) may be unable to voluntarily move his legs, but they will still be reflexively responsive to positioning such that they may go into spasm or contraction even though the individual cannot "feel" them. With respect to sexual functioning, the matter is slightly more complex.

Male and Female Neurophysiology

Erections in the male are of two basic types: reflexogenic and psychogenic. These categories are neither discrete nor mutually exclusive. Both are involved in sexual response.

Reflexogenic erections are not cortically mediated and involve the sacral 2 to 4 (S2 to S4) segments of the cord. The reflex arc involved uses only the parasympathetic nervous system so that if physical stimulation to the general genital area is not maintained, neither will the erection be maintained. These types of erections can occur independently of any conscious awareness and may occur in response to a full bladder, casual touch or stimulation, or the introduction of a catheter. For the individual whose injury is above the sacral area, these types of erections are most probable.

Psychogenic or psychic erections are those that are mediated through the cortex. Stimuli resulting in erection may be auditory, visual, kinesthetic, olfactory, or imaginal, and may not involve genital areas directly. This is the type of erection that commonly results when a male is sexually aroused. Neurophysiologically, the cortical impulses travel from the brain and exit between the thoracic 9 and lumbar 2 cord segments. These impulses also involve the sympathetic nervous system. Comparing the two types of erectile processes, one can deduce that spinal injured males generally are able to have reflexogenic erections when their injury is not in the sacral area of the cord, and may experience psychogenic erections when injuries do occur in this area. Despite the anatomical issues involved, it is important to reiterate that arousal and response patterns are not merely neurophysiological events. Able-bodied and spinal injured alike have developed their own idiosyncratic styles of responding sexually. These must be dealt with in the course of any sexual adjustment counseling.

Problems of erectile functioning in the SCI male may be the result of both physiological and psychological difficulties. The individual's neurophysiological response may result in diminished sensitivity to begin with, so that other forms of stimulation to other body areas may be necessary. With respect to reflexogenic response, stimulation must generally be maintained for erection to continue. This often requires adjustment between the individual and his partner. Psychological issues such as self-image, communication, confidence, attitude, and knowledge are also likely to play an important role in enhancing or detracting from the individual's capability for responding, especially with regard to psychogenic erection, although all sexual responses are likely to be affected.

Emission in the male is a function of the sympathetic nervous system. Sensory impulses originate in the pelvic area and travel to the cord via the internal pudendal nerve. Motor impulses in response originate in the cord between the thoracic 11 and lumbar 3 segments and eventually innervate the epididymus, vas deferens, and the prostate so that sperm and supporting fluid are produced just a few seconds prior to orgasm.

The emission of semen into the posterior path to the urethra triggers both a reflexogenic and psychogenic response. Sacral 2 to 4 as well as thoracic 9 to lumbar 3 segments are involved with the ultimate outcome of contraction and ejaculation. When this process is disrupted, as in the spinal injured, retrograde ejaculation may occur whereby semen flows backward into the bladder. This will be discussed later.

Orgasm in the male is primarily a cerebral event, although there are obvious correlates with emission and ejaculation, especially in the able-bodied male. In spinal injured males, however, this relationship between subjective experience of orgasm and ejaculation may be quite different. Whereas "phantom orgasm," as described by Comarr (1970) and Money (1960), may be somewhat imprecise and inaccurate, it is entirely possible for the spinal injured person to experience strong, pleasurable feelings without the process of ejaculation. Comarr and Vigue (1978) reported a significant relationship between orgasmic ability and ability to fantasize in both men and women with complete lesions.

Neurophysiologically, the female response is similar to the male's in that it is mediated in the pelvis by the same nerves. These consist of fibers from the lowest sympathetic ganglia, the presacral parasympathetics and the sensory and motor fibers of the pudendal nerve. The effect of spinal injury on the female follows a similar pattern.

In the excitement phase, female physiological response involves vascular engorgement, which results in vaginal lubrication, labial engorgement, and clitoral erection. Other nongenital responses occur, such as nipple erection and initial breast engorgement. General systemic changes such as increased blood pressure and heart rate are likely to occur.

With continued excitement, the plateau phase is initiated, with concomitant changes in vagina, labia, and clitoris. Increased breast engorgement and blood flow to the periphery may result in flushing of the chest, neck, and face.

Orgasmic experiences for able-bodied females generally involve rhythmic contractions of the uterus and vaginal walls with overall increases in muscle tension, blood pressure, and heart rate. During resolution, there is gradual detumescence of the pelvic area unless more stimulation is applied.

Notably, in some females, there is no latency period following orgasm and multiple orgasms are possible.

The effect of the lesion in spinal injury will depend in part on whether it is an upper or lower motor neuron lesion. Upper motor neurons originate in the brain and carry impulses to different areas of the cord. Lower motor neurons originate in the cord itself and travel outward to different muscles, etc. They are the links between the cord and the structures they innervate. Injury to the cord will disrupt these neurons in different ways. Upper and lower motor neurons above the level of injury remain intact but those below may be disrupted. Upper motor neurons connected to areas below the site of injury will be disrupted since the connections are likely to be affected at the site of injury. Lower motor neurons below the area of injury are not likely to be influenced since these are primarily involved in reflexive response. The sacral segments are used as a reference for classifying upper or lower motor neuron functioning. Those injuries above the sacral area are classified as upper motor neuron (UMN), and those at or below it, lower motor neuron (LMN). UMN injuries result in spastic, hyperreflexive (overreactive) conditions. Sexually, males are likely to achieve erection but not necessarily ejaculation or orgasm. LMN individuals generally have a flaccid areflexic type of functioning. They may experience ejaculation and have a psychological feeling of orgasm. There is little reliable data on female response, but what is available indicates that women with complete UMN lesions appear to be able to develop sensitivity to other erogenous zones to compensate for the lack of genital stimulation. Stimulation above the area of the lesion may result in a type of orgasmic experience discussed earlier. This finding has been corroborated by Bregman and Hadley (1976) and Money (1960).

Fertility, as it relates to UMN and LMN lesions, has been studied by Bors and Comarr (1960). They report that fertility for males may range from 1% in the incomplete upper motor neuron group to 10% in the incomplete lower motor neuron group. This is due, in part, to the lowered number of ejaculations as compared to erections; retrograde ejaculations are also part of the problem. The disruption of thoracic 12 to lumbar 1 segments allows the sperm to flow into the bladder, where it is destroyed by the acidity of the urine. Female fertility is generally unaffected by spinal injury.

Therapists who deal with spinal injured individuals should be aware of the neurophysiological features just discussed. They should also be aware of the exceptions that occur throughout the literature. There is no substitute, however, for empirically based, technically correct information in dealing with any disabled individual.

Other issues affecting sexuality have also been studied. The spinal cord injured person's sense of self, self-concept, and self-esteem are likely to be profoundly influenced by the injury (Lovitt, 1970; Singh & Magner, 1975). This change in image no doubt affects sexuality. In order to compensate for changes in perceived physical attractiveness, new emphasis may be placed on appearance and communication style so as to enhance approachability (Berscheid & Walster, 1974). The relationship between positive self-image and sexual adjustment was described by Bregman and Hadley (1976) in a study with female spinal cord injured individuals. Bogle and Shaul (1981) emphasized the importance of dealing with body image and its implications for the disabled woman. Three excellent source books by Trieschman (1980), Rabin (1980), and Bullard and Knight (1981) provide overviews of other issues that are related to sexuality and spinal injury.

HEART DISEASE

The fear of a heart attack brought on by sexual activity has been one of the primary reasons that many cardiac patients have given up this aspect of their lives. A careful perusal of the data, however, indicates that this may be an unwarranted course of action. Wagner (1975) discusses several studies that have shed needed empirical light on this area. In the normal male, sexual activity is associated with variable cardiovascular changes: heart rates may range from 110 to 180 beats per minute; blood pressure may increase 40 to 80 mm, systolic, and 20 to 50 mm, diastolic; and respiration rates may range from 30 to 60 respirations per minute.

Hellerstein and Friedman (1970) indicate that, overall, the physiological cost of sexual activity on the middle-aged, long-married male is modest, with all factors being considered. In commenting on this study, Wagner indicated the advisability of adequate counseling of the cardiac-prone individual in various practical matters, such as sexual positioning, as a way of decreasing excessive cardiovascular stress.

The notion of the danger of heart attack during intercourse has also been examined by Hellerstein and Friedman, who maintain that the probability is actually quite low. In general, death from heart problems has generally occurred in situations (or with persons) that were already stress-laden for other reasons. Practical issues, such as familiarity with a partner and premorbid sexual style, were also examined.

Masturbation can be a most effective way of reintroducing sexuality to the cardiac patient. This approach, of course, assumes that such activity will be viewed as pleasurable and not guilt producing. Wagner (1975) again presents data indicating that perhaps initial self-stimulation is not as physiologically taxing as intercourse and may, in fact, better prepare the patient for it by gradual desensitization with respect to the fear that coitus might engender.

Another aspect of this issue involves drug effects and sexual response. This is especially relevant for individuals using antihypertensive medication. There is much variability in what patients are told regarding the possible implications of medication and their sexual response (Renshaw, 1978). Kolodny (1978) presents pertinent information on a commonly used drug, alpha-methyldopa, and its effect on sexuality in males. He indicated that 36 of 105 subjects (34.3%) reported diminished sexual functioning after inception of antihypertensive treatment with this drug. Laver (1974) and Newman and Salerno (1974) reported similar findings with antihypertensives. Treatment of the sexual aspects of the hypertensive drug issue has ranged from reduction of dosage to initiation of sex therapy. Kolodny points out the importance not only of ascertaining the physiological aspects of the problem but also dealing with the obvious psychosocial concerns of patients.

As noted previously, the primary concern of the cardiac-prone individual is that intense sexual activity may result in a heart attack. Other concerns, however, may revolve around changes in perceived competence, body image, self-concept, and physical attractiveness. The role of the partner is also one that of necessity must be explored if appropriate and effective counseling is to proceed (Mackey, 1978).

OTHER DISORDERS

Literature now exists that deals with the sexual concerns of individuals with a wide variety of disorders. Space constraints prevent the detailed discussion of each. We will offer a brief synopsis of the primary concerns and available resources for each disorder, with the suggestion that further reading in the specific area will enhance awareness and understanding.

Renal Disease

Hemodialysis has allowed many end-stage renal disease patients to remain alive for considerable lengths of time. Along with this increased longevity has come the concern for continued sexual activity. Levy (1978) addresses this issue in direct forms. Scribner (1974) reported the occurrence of impotence in hemodialysis males as 33%. Friedman, Goodwin, and Chaudry (1970) and McKevitt (1976) suggest the importance of dealing with the psychological reactions of patients to the organic features that may contribute to sexual dysfunction.

Diabetes

Sexual dysfunction has been one of the unfortunate consequences of diabetes mellitus in both men and women (Kolodny, Kahn, Goldstein, & Barnett, 1978). There have been several arguments as to the specific etiological causes, including vascular problems, other systemic diseases, and psychological factors (Masters & Johnson, 1970). Much of the research work has been done with males; there is at least one study (Kolodny, 1971) that, although dated, gives some insight into the problems of female diabetics. For males suffering from impotence, with an organic etiology, prosthetics have been advised, whereas with mixed clinical presentations, other therapeutic approaches are more appropriate. The decisions are often difficult to make, since clear etiological features are often difficult to ascertain.

Arthritis

The significant sexuality-related issues of the arthritic are most likely to involve mobility, pain, and body image. Ehrlich (1978) has discussed these issues in detail, as have Katz (1977) and Swinburn (1976). Despite the obvious mechanical interference the disease may present with regard to sexual functioning, it is probably the psychological features that require the most intervention. Depression, dependency, poor self-image, and avoidance of interpersonal contact may characterize the response of the arthritic individual who has not developed appropriate coping skills, either before onset or in response to the disease. Specific treatment approaches to deal with these issues will be discussed fully in the treatment model segment that follows.

Sexuality research has also been conducted with regard to multiple sclerosis (Vas, 1978); stroke (Renshaw, 1978); and mastectomy (Green & Mantell, 1978), to name but a few disorders. The point here has not been to name all of the disorders that have been studied, but rather to raise the reader's awareness that much more is being done, and needs to be done, to deal more fully with the sexual needs of the disabled. References are merely sources of information by which the therapist fortifies his or her own understanding of the problems faced by patients. The next section deals with the practical aspects of therapeutic intervention.

TREATMENT CONSIDERATIONS

Many treatment models have been offered that purportedly deal with the sexual concerns of the disabled (Anon, 1974; Brockway & Steger, 1978; Cole, Chilgren, & Rosenberg, 1973). The importance of appropriate response to the sexual adjustment needs of the disabled has been likewise emphasized (Baxter & Linn, 1978; Cole, 1975). The actual response of the therapist to the patient and his or her family will, of course, be a function of many variables that are idiosyncratic to particular treatment situations. The practical approach presented here draws from a number of sources, including the clinical experience of the authors, in order to demonstrate the general phases of dealing with sex and disability.

The first aspect of sexual therapy or adjustment counseling with the disabled has to do not with the patient but with the therapist. Cole (1975) and others have strongly emphasized the importance of thoroughly exploring one's own attitudes regarding disability and sexuality before embarking on a therapeutic journey with a patient. The therapist's comfort level with what is discussed may shape the ultimate outcome of the therapeutic intervention, for better or worse!

Clearly, sexual functioning is a legitimate and important concern in the context of rehabilitation. Appropriate sexual adjustment is both a process and a goal. It is a process in that it involves the disabled person and significant others in a concerted effort to improve or enhance functioning in an appropriate manner, and a goal in that the ability to perform sexually in a comfortable and pleasurable manner will contribute to overall psychological well-being, the ultimate goal of all efforts.

Initiation of sexual adjustment counseling may occur at any point in time. The primary limiting factor generally is the patient's readiness, which, in this case, refers to the patient's comfort level and willingness to discuss sexual concerns. The first therapeutic task becomes the building of appropriate rapport and putting the patient at ease. These can be accomplished in a wide range of ways: communicating a sense of understanding and nonjudgmental acceptance of the patient's concern; effective listening on the part of the therapist to really hear what is being said or communicated in other ways; and explicit giving of permission to the patient by the therapist to actively question, explore, or pursue sexual concerns. The product of these therapeutic skills is a validation of the other person's experience, so critical especially in the initial stages of therapeutic contact. The most logical and practical vehicle for beginning the process is the initial interview.

Assessment

The importance of the initial contact with the disabled person cannot be overemphasized, since it may set the stage for what happens next in the counseling process. Information may be elicited from several sources, including the patient. Care should be taken, of course, with respect to confidentiality issues. The patient's consent is always to be solicited before information is requested from other sources.

The content of the initial interview may vary according to situation, but there are some general guidelines that should be followed. The type of information elicited with respect to the patient's physiological functioning might include:

- gross sensory and motor functions or impairments
- system review with regard to premorbid and/or related problems
- pain levels and locations
- fatigue and endurance concerns
- general and specific sexual response mechanisms

A second important aspect of the initial interview is ascertaining the patient's psychosocial assets and deficits with respect to potential adjustment counseling. Issues that might arise during this phase of the interview include:

- patient's motivation for treatment
- premorbid personality style
- past and current stress levels
- stress coping skills
- perceived level of adjustment to injury or disease
- importance of significant others to the patient and their role
- premorbid interpersonal skills
- level of comfort with body image
- level of satisfaction with overall functioning
- specific sexual performance concerns

A third aspect of the initial contact may deal directly with the individual's sexual attitudes and beliefs. This may be the most delicate of the three assessment elements to handle, given the presenting complaint. Some individuals simply do not like to discuss their sexual functioning with anyone and may need more time to become more comfortable with the therapist. If this does not appear to be a significant issue, the type of information most helpful to acquire is:

- cultural beliefs
- religious beliefs
- sexual preferences
- premorbid sexual history
- knowledge of and comfort level with assistance devices (vibrators, etc.)
- history of sexual relationships and priorities
- male-female sex role issues
- self-image and sexual attractiveness

There also exist some excellent paper-and-pencil questionnaires that are useful for acquiring information in less direct fashion. These include the Sexual Attitude and Information Questionnaire (SAIQ) for spinal injured individuals (Brockway & Steger, 1978) and the Sexual Interaction Inventory (SII) by LoPiccolo and Steger (1974).

Information may also be obtained through a comprehensive sexological examination performed by a physician. Indeed this may be useful in affording the patient an opening to discuss sexual concerns. Other sources of important data may be gleaned from the patient's medical history or physician with respect to any other physiological factors, such as hereditary, hormonal, perceptual, or systemic factors.

Information Giving and Goal Planning

Once the data have been collected, the next step involves the identification of issues for intervention. During this phase of treatment, the patient and therapist explore the possibilities for action that have turned up during the evaluation process. The patient's concerns regarding physical mobility, fear of dependency, and poor self-image may be identified as potential areas of intervention. During this phase the therapist also provides limited information about the concerns mentioned, so as to pace the patient's growing knowledge and understanding without overwhelming him or her with facts and figures. The emphasis is upon the patient's expressing his or her concerns and communicating a willingness to work on them.

The therapist's role at this stage of treatment is to assist the patient in prioritizing his or her areas of concern. The therapist may act as a resource person in giving technically correct information to the patient so as to enhance the patient's ability to set reasonable goals in the prioritized areas. Another therapist role is to help the patient recognize any deficits he or she brings to the situation and discuss ways of reversing these deficits. For example, a patient may insist that the primary problem in being unable to establish a satisfactory sexual relationship is due to his or her problems with physical mobility but may deny the significant implications of deficiencies in social skills identified by the therapist. Issues such as these become the dynamic aspects of the ongoing therapeutic relationship. Oftentimes, negotiations may be in order with respect to what will be worked on primarily and secondarily and so on. The prevailing concern on the part of the therapist must be twofold: respect for the patient's right to self-determination and acceptance of the patient's ultimate responsibility for change.

In addition to contact with the patient, the therapist may also meet with significant others to enlist their help in planning interventions as well as to assist them in their adjustment process. It is extremely important to learn from partners what their beliefs, attitudes, and perceived goals are with respect to the patient. Information in the form of written materials and films is made as available to them as to the patient. One of the greatest tragedies in treatment occurs when significant others are not directly involved in the treatment process and thus are totally unprepared to deal with the patient when he or she is ready to actively deal with relevant concerns.

Active Treatment

Once the patient has identified the specific goals he or she will work on, the next step is taken. This involves active participation in a systematic treatment program. The therapist now draws upon his or her expertise in providing specific suggestions to the patient and the significant other with respect to the concerns identified. These suggestions are evaluated as to performance and ultimate impact on the targeted behavior. For example, a diabetic may be asked to engage in pleasuring exercises with the partner as a way of reestablishing physical contact without the demand of intercourse. Feedback from the patient and the significant other is crucial to ensure that suggestions are being followed correctly.

This is often the phase in which new forms of sexual behavior are attempted. They might include the use of assistance devices such as vibrators; attempts at other sexual positions; or alternative methods, such as manual or oral sexual pleasuring. All suggestions are given in the context of knowledge of the patient and the significant other's personal resources. Information and suggestions are provided only as the patient's capabilities warrant. Issues such as performance anxiety and "spectatoring" are discussed and dealt with as they relate to the ongoing process.

It is important to see the aforementioned process as an interrelated schema as opposed to a lock-step format. Patients and significant others may cycle through the process several times as new issues arise and are dealt with. The following case example illustrates some of the basic features:

> Bill is a 21-year-old male who suffered a C5-6 fracture dislocation in an automobile accident. He immediately became quadriplegic with complete loss of strength below C6 and partial sensory sparing below that level. Because the lesion was incomplete, he had partial use of his hands. At the time of admission to a rehabilitation hospital several weeks after injury, sacral sensation was present but diminished, voluntary anal sphincter control was absent, and bulbocavernosus and ano-cutaneous reflexes were hypoactive. Bill indicated that he had genital sensation and had experienced erections when his external catheter was applied. He said that he had asked his neurosurgeon about his prognosis and had been told that he would never be able to have sex again. Bill was then provided with the information that many spinal cord injured men are able to have satisfying sexual relationships. He was encouraged to get to know his new body and to explore it in terms of areas of pleasant sensation, diminished sensation, dysesthesias, and absent sensation.
>
> Approximately two weeks after admission, Bill met with his physiatrist to discuss aspects of his management. He described his experiences with self-exploration since hospitalization and was given further information and reassurance regarding the sexual capacities of spinal cord injured men. Bill was eager to further explore his sexual capacities.
>
> A meeting was then held with Candy, a young woman with whom Bill was intending to live following discharge. She wanted very much to spend the night with Bill. She felt that she was in love with him, but feared that if things didn't work out sexually, the relationship would be doomed. Candy was given basic information, reassurance regarding the normalcy of her concerns, and permission to take care of her own needs as well as Bill's.
>
> Six weeks into the rehabilitation program, Bill and Candy first stayed overnight in their apartment. Afterwards Bill reported that he had been

preoccupied with when to take his external catheter off and how often to put it back on again. He was pleased that he did not wet the bed, had no involuntary bowel movements, and remembered to turn his body to prevent bed sores. Candy had been worried about losing the spontaneity of sex and concerned that having to assist Bill physically would detract from the romance of the moment. Nonetheless, Candy experienced orgasm for the first time in her life, following oral stimulation by Bill. They also had successful intercourse but without ejaculation or orgasm for Bill. After several more sessions in their apartment, Bill was reporting occasional orgasm and ejaculation. His ability to feel in the genital area was much less intense than before the accident; however, his erections lasted indefinitely, as long as stimulation continued. After ejaculation, continued stimulation led to several orgasms in a row. Candy was elated, since she was regularly orgasmic with Bill. They had some questions about their potential for having a child and a semen analysis was recommended.

After 18 weeks, Bill was ready for discharge. He had reached his goals in mobility, self-care, bowel and bladder management, and psychological and vocational rehabilitation.

After discharge, Bill and Candy were seen several times in follow-up. They were both working. They continued to have a good sexual relationship. They felt that the opportunities they had for sexual exploration during his hospitalization strengthened their relationship, and contributed to his overall positive attitude about himself and to his success in the rehabilitation program.

Bill and Candy's case is one of many that the authors have seen in clinical practice. There were obvious advantages, not seen in all cases, in working with this bright, young, motivated couple. The process of working with all individuals is similar, however, in that the goal is satisfactory sexual functioning, as defined by the individual.

CONCLUSION

Much of the effectiveness of therapy will depend on the extent to which treatment encompasses the disabled individual's significant relationships, that is, with an intimate partner or spouse and family. Treatment formats must be flexible to permit individual, couple, and family sessions as needed. Major guidelines have been posited for the general phases of therapy—assessment, information giving and goal planning, and active treatment. Prior to actual treatment, however, two prerequisites for the therapist are crucial: (1) accurate knowledge of the patient's specific disability and (2) competence in sexual counseling, including a comfort level based on awareness of one's own sexuality. Beyond these principles, intervention approaches must be selected to meet the idiosyncratic needs of each patient. For example, some may require considerable time working through self-image and self-concept issues; others may need to focus on the impact of the disability on family roles, dynamics, and relationships; and still others may need attention in an immediate crisis, for example, the prospect of divorce, brought on or exacerbated by the disability and its sequelae.

As disabled people continue to demand their sexual rights, significant gains in the systematic study of sexuality and disability should follow. Hopefully, this specialized information and research will lead to more effective and efficient interventions for individuals, couples, and families.

REFERENCES

Anon, J. *The behavioral treatment of sexual problems* (Vol. 1), *Brief therapy*. Honolulu: Kapiolan Health Systems, 1974.

Baxter, R., & Linn, A. Sexual counseling and the SCI patient. *Nursing*, 1978, *78*, 46-52.

Berkman, A., Weissman, R., & Frielich, M. Sexual adjustment of spinal cord injured veterans living in the community. *Archives of Physical Medicine and Rehabilitation*, 1978, *59*, 29-33.

Berscheid, E., & Walster, E. Physical attractiveness. *Advances in Experimental Social Psychology*, 1974, *7*, 157-215.

Bogle, J., & Shaul, S. Body image and the woman with a disability. In D. Bullard & S. Knight (Eds.), *Sexuality and physical disability*. St. Louis: C.V. Mosby, 1981.

Bors, E., & Comarr, A. Neurological disturbances of sexual function with special reference to 529 patients with spinal cord injury. *Urological Survey*, 1960, *10*, 191-222.

Bregman, S., & Hadley, R. Sexual adjustment and feminine attractiveness among spinal injured women. *Archives of Physical Medicine and Rehabilitation*, 1976, *57*, 448-450.

Brockway, J., & Steger, J. *Sexual attitude and information questionnaire: Reliability and validity in a spinal cord injured population.* Paper presented at meeting of the American Congress of Rehabilitation Medicine, New Orleans, November, 1978.

Bullard, D., & Knight, S. (Eds.). *Sexuality and physical disability*. St. Louis: C.V. Mosby, 1981.

Cole, T. Sexuality and physical disabilities. *Archives of Sexual Behavior*, 1975, *4*, 389-403.

Cole, T., Chilgren, R., & Rosenberg, P. A new programme of sex education and counseling for spinal cord injured adults and health care professionals. *International Journal of Paraplegia*, 1973, *11*, 111-124.

Cole, T., & Cole, S. The handicapped and sexual health. In A. Comfort (Ed.), *Sexual consequences of disability*. Philadelphia: George F. Stickley, 1978.

Comarr, A. Sexual function among patients with spinal cord injury. *Urology Interviews*, 1970, *25*, 134-168.

Comarr, A., & Vigue, M. Sexual counseling among male and female patients with spinal cord and/or cauda equina injury, Part 1. *American Journal of Physical Medicine*, 1978, *57*, 102-122.

Corbet, B. *Options: Spinal cord injury and the future.* Denver: A.B. Hirschfeld, 1980.

Ehrlich, G. Sexual problems of the arthritic. In A. Comfort (Ed.), *Sexual consequences of disability*. Philadelphia: George F. Stickley, 1978.

Friedman, E.A., Goodwin, N., & Chaudry, L. Psychosocial adjustment of family to maintenance hemodialysis, Part II. *N.Y. State Journal of Medicine*, 1970, *70*, 767.

Green, C., & Mantell, J. The need for management of the psychosocial aspects of mastectomy. In A. Comfort (Ed.), *Sexual consequences of disability*. Philadelphia: George F. Stickley, 1978.

Hellerstein, H., & Friedman, E. Sexual activity and the post-coronary patient. *Archives of Internal Medicine*, 1970, *125*, 987-999.

Hohmann, G. Consideration in management of psychosexual adjustment in the cord injured male. *Rehabilitation Psychology*, 1972, *19*, 50-58.

Katz, W. Sexuality and arthritis. In W. Katz (Ed.), *Rheumatic diseases: Diagnosis and management*. Philadelphia: J.B. Lippincott, 1977.

Kolodny, R. Sexual dysfunction in diabetic females. *Journal of American Diabetes Association*, 1971, *20*, 557-559.

Kolodny, R. Effects of alpha-methyldopa on male sexual function. *Sexuality and Disability*, 1978, *1*, 223-228.

Kolodny, R., Kahn, L., Goldstein, H., & Barnett, D. Sexual dysfunction in diabetic men. In A. Comfort (Ed.), *Sexual consequences of disability*. Philadelphia: George F. Stickley, 1978.

Laver, M. Sexual behavior patterns in male hypertensives. *Australia and New Zealand Journal of Medicine*, 1974, *4*, 29-31.

Levy, N. Psychological studies on hemodialysis patients at the Downstate Medical Center. *Medical Clinics of North America*, 1977, *61*, 759.

Levy, N. Sexual function in hemodialysis patients. In A. Comfort (Ed.), *Sexual consequences of disability*. Philadelphia: George F. Stickley, 1978.

LoPiccolo, J., & Steger, J. The sexual interaction inventory: A new instrument for assessment of sexual dysfunction. *Archives of Sexual Behavior*, 1974, *3*, 585-595.

Lovitt, R. Sexual adjustment of spinal cord injury patients. *Rehabilitation Research and Practice Review*, 1970, *1*, 25-29.

Mackey, F. Sexuality and heart disease. In A. Comfort (Ed.), *Sexual consequences of disability*. Philadelphia: George F. Stickley, 1978.

Masters, W., & Johnson, V. *Human sexual inadequacy*. Boston: Little, Brown, 1970.

McKevitt, P. Treating sexual dysfunction in dialysis and transplantation patients. *Health and Social Work*, 1976, *1*, 133-157.

Money, J. Phantom orgasm in the dreams of paraplegic men and women. *Archives of General Psychiatry*, 1960, *3*, 373-382.

Newman, R., & Salerno, H. Sexual dysfunction due to methyldopa. *British Medical Journal*, 1974, *106*, 4.

Rabin, B.J. *The sensuous wheeler: Sexual adjustment for the spinal cord injured.* San Francisco: Multi Media Resource Center, 1980.

Renshaw, D. Stroke and sex. In A. Comfort (Ed.), *Sexual consequences of disability.* Philadelphia: George F. Stickley, 1978.

Scribner, B. Panel discussion. In N. Levy (Ed.), *Living or dying: Adaptation to hemodialysis.* Springfield: Charles C Thomas, 1974.

Singh, S., & Magner, T. Sex and self: The spinal cord injured. *Rehabilitation Literature,* 1975, *36,* 2-10.

Swinburn, W. Sexual counseling for the arthritic. In V. Wright (Ed.), *Rheumatic diseases diagnosis and management.* Philadelphia: J.B. Lippincott, 1976.

Trieschman, R. *Spinal cord injuries: Psychological, social and vocational adjustment.* New York: Pergamon Press, 1980.

Vas, C. Sexual impotence and some autonomic disorders in men with multiple sclerosis. In A. Comfort (Ed.), *Sexual consequences of disability.* Philadelphia: George F. Stickley, 1978.

Wagner, N. Sexual activity and the cardiac patient. In R. Green (Ed.), *Human sexuality: A health practitioners text.* Baltimore: Williams & Wilkins, 1975.

8. Ethical and Legal Aspects of Sexual Issues

Robert Henley Woody, PhD, ScD, JD
Professor
Psychology Department
University of Nebraska at Omaha
Omaha, Nebraska

SEX IN FAMILY THERAPY SEEMS TO BE LIKE SEX IN EVERYDAY LIFE —there is typically more talk about it than action. Family therapists deal constantly with sex in one form or another, yet it is the rare professional training program that provides systematic preparation for handling sexual matters. Likewise, licensure and certification plans seldom give formal recognition to the pronounced role that sex plays in treatment. Instead of licensing or certifying sex therapy, preference is given to a broad discipline, such as psychology or social work (which could allow for a license or certification without adequate training in the critical dimension of sex). Finally, professional codes of ethics have shown reluctance to specify contacts with clients as being unethical; proscriptions have been prudently couched in the language of general care for the client, as opposed to delineating sexual acts as being ethically inappropriate.

Fortunately, despite the continuing avoidance of specificity about sex in professional-client relationships, a few professional organizations have stepped forward; for example, the American Psychological Association's "Ethical Principles of Psychologists" (1981) now states: "Psychologists make every effort to avoid dual relationships that could impair their professional judgment or increase the risk of exploitation. . . . Sexual intimacies with clients are unethical" (p. 636).

This article will focus on the following areas: preparation for the family therapist to deal with sexuality properly; the pervasiveness of sexual matters in family therapy; and ethical and legal issues inherent in providing sex-related therapy. The end goal is a practitioner's frame of reference for ethical and legal functioning.

EDUCATION AND TRAINING

Traditionally, family therapist educators and trainers have asserted that sex is not a discrete area of the curriculum; they have argued that content on human sexuality should be integrated into core courses. Occasionally, a more advanced techniques course has included coverage of procedures with applicability to sexual matters; but in general, sex problems per se have been considered to be beyond general training and to be a treatment area that should remain in the province of the specialist with postgraduate training.

Postgraduate training has often been limited as well, for there have been only sparse opportunities for even the seasoned family therapist to obtain training that would truly form a comprehensive specialization. The result, as might be expected, has been a coterie of family therapists who chanced upon practical experiences or isolated academic learning that allow them the self-assurance to move into treatments avoided by therapists with less preparation.

With the advent of the certification programs for Sex Educator, Sex Counselor, and Sex Therapist promulgated by the American Association of Sex Educators, Counselors, and Therapists (AASECT), the need for education and training experiences to ensure at least a minimal degree of academic and clinical competency has been recognized. These ideas are still embryonic in the overall education and training framework, but they will lead to improved opportunities for professional preparation.

License and certification programs have yet to move decisively or consistently to specify training in sexuality, yet there is some recognition that such training could be a legitimate credential for justifying a state's statutory endorsement (or that of a professional association). For example, Florida's statute for licensure of marriage and family counselors specifies that:

> Every applicant for licensure as a marriage and family counselor shall verify the required supervised experience by demonstrating one or more of the following: (a) Evidence of being a clinical member of the American Association for Marriage and Family Therapy Register. (b) Evidence of being a sex counselor or therapist in the Register of the American Association of Sex Educators, Counselors, and Therapists. (F.S. 21U-500.04)

Although a license could still be obtained without education and training in sex therapy, such preparation has been recognized as being equivalent to more traditional preparation approaches. This, too, marks a good beginning.

TRANSFERENCE AND COUNTERTRANSFERENCE

When family therapist educators and trainers have been concerned about a trainee's ability to handle sexual matters properly, it has usually been viewed from the standpoint of transference and countertransference.

Early Freudian theory and its numerous derivations have asserted that a client is apt to develop—indeed can therapeutically benefit from experiencing—transference toward the therapist. In transference, the client responds to the affective intimacy of the therapy by projecting onto the family therapist qualities that are not actually present—there is a transference of some other person's (real or fantasy) characteristics to the therapist. These can be positive or negative attributions, but (of concern for this discussion) they can easily be sexual in nature. That is, there are feelings and perceptions on the part of the client that could transform platonic therapeutic interactions into sexualized ones. These can be healthy, but only if the family therapist is able to confront the transference-based responses in a constructive manner. However, if sexual transference is allowed to go beyond the therapeutic relationship and to become reality (acting out), the results can mean denigration of the tenets of treatment and represent potential harm to the client.

Conversely, the family therapist is apt to experience feelings for and perceptions toward the client that are not, in fact, generated by the client per se. Rather, they come from the therapist's apperceptive mass of experiences with others and his or her psychological need system. This countertransference has been the concern of family therapist educators and trainers, but like so many areas of clinical preparation, the monitoring of the development of competency to handle transference and countertransference has been limited at best.

The professional literature is replete with advocacy for all therapists to obtain the degree of self-understanding requisite for ensuring that the client's needs are paramount, that the needs of the therapist are well controlled, and that therapists act only in the service of the client (not for their own ego or need fulfillment). Shoben (1965) urges an "examined life," and Arnold (1967) recommends counseling for trainees to provide them with an opportunity to acquire self-understanding. Such self-insight does seem to correlate with the ability to facilitate conditions that will promote therapeutic progress in clients (Woody, 1971). Unfortunately, choosing a career as a therapist does not ensure or guarantee any high degree of this crucial qualification (Arbuckle, 1966; Mezzano, 1968).

The failure to be prepared for constructively handling transference and countertransference responses is the basis for the occasions of sexual relations between therapists and clients. Because of the nature of the activities, there are no reliable and valid means for determining the extent to which sexual relations are acted out within the context of treatment. Rather than pursue ill-defined statistics, suffice it to say that even surveys that are admittedly restricted in their ability to verify such sexual occurrences support the statement that a significant amount of sexual activity does occur between therapists and clients (Masters, Johnson, & Kolodny, 1977).

While the nature and extent of therapist-client sexual relations cannot be definitively stated, it seems certain that the therapy is compromised when sexual acts occur between persons who were brought together in a professional context. That is, therapy by definition (be it from theory or by societal endorsement) does not sanction sexual activities between the therapist and client.

ETHICAL AND LEGAL ISSUES

Sexual relations between a family therapist and client potentially constitute a violation of ethics and, quite likely, the law. It should be understood that therapy ceases when transference and countertransference are improperly treated, and that allowing sexual relations to occur in the therapeutic context is unequivocally a breach of professionalism.

The ethical and legal nature of sexual relations between therapist and client has received formal recognition. We have already mentioned the code of ethics of the American Psychological Association. Furthermore, it is not unusual for a state licensure or certification program to incorporate a code of ethics into the statutory language, for example, saying that maintenance of the "Ethical Principles of Psychologists" of the American Psychological Association is a prerequisite for holding licensure as a psychologist. In Florida, for example, the statute indicates that disciplinary action will be taken (including denial of a license either temporarily or permanently) if, among other possible acts, there is:

(k) Committing any act upon a patient or client, other than the spouse of the actor, which would constitute sexual battery, or which would constitute sexual misconduct. . . . (F.S. 490.009)

As might be assumed, the legal consequences can go beyond impact upon the licensure or certification. The client (or public prosecutor) has the right to bring charges under either criminal or civil law (depending upon the circumstances). Thus the penalties can be personal and professional humiliation, monetary damages, and even incarceration.

For the specialization of sex therapist, the   AASECT Code of Ethics (1978) is even more specific with various proscriptions that restrict sexual situations; these include the following:

A sex therapist will not use his or her therapeutic relationship to further personal . . . interests (p. 13)

It is unethical for the therapist to engage in sexual activity with a client (p. 13)

Procedures involving nudity of either the client or the therapist or observation of client sexual activity go beyond the boundaries of established therapeutic practice . . . (p. 13)

. . . Sex therapists working with partner surrogates must exercise diligence and concern for protecting the dignity and welfare of both the surrogate and the client (p. 15).

Note that AASECT maintains numerous criteria that define the controversial use of partner surrogates in sex therapy. Without strict adherence to these criteria, an ethical violation would be incurred.

PROFESSIONAL LIABILITY

Failure to fulfill ethical and legal requirements can result in sanctions. If the matter is purely ethical, i.e., there is no violation of a client's civil rights or of a statutory law, it will remain for a professional organization to obtain a remedy. This typically involves a series of reviews by professional committees, and rarely leads to a penalty beyond the distress inflicted by the committee sessions (of course, the expense of having legal representation throughout the review procedures can become a penalty of sorts). Even with religiouslike respect for professionalism, there is often a reluctance to battle with one's colleagues and to follow through to total resolution of the matter. Committees tend to wish to find an escape route that will allow a "saving of face" for all parties. Similarly, clients—even if clearly wronged—are reluctant to attack professionals, especially one who was at one time a helper; consequently, many legal actions are threatened but are not brought to fruition.

When a legal action is brought against a therapist, it seldom becomes a full-blown court case. Wright (1981) indicates that ". . . the majority (more than 75%) of claims against psychologists fall in the nuisance category (i.e., they are settled for less than $5,000, including legal costs)" (p. 1538). He also points out how important it is to have an effective system for handling fees, commenting: "Without getting into the technicalities of what this does to the patient-practitioner relationship, it is a fact that malpractice actions are frequently initiated at the point where the practitioner begins to demand payment" (p. 1540).

A nuisance suit is not reduced in its psychological and financial impact simply because it is ill founded. The family therapist who has acted in good faith and maintained an acceptable standard of care will still be vulnerable to the devastating effects of being accused of malpractice. When the ill-founded allegations are sexual in nature, the negative consequences—even though no ethical or legal violation has been documented—can affect the professional's reputation within both the community and the discipline.

CONFIDENTIALITY

Too many family therapists believe that they cannot speak out when they are accused of malpractice, that is, they are concerned about violating the accusing client's rights. From a legal point of view, this is not the case. Once a client enters into a dispute with a professional, protective confidentiality is waived by the client. For example, the client who is lax in paying a fee cannot expect the family therapist to refuse to "go public" about having served the client. While seeking payment for the services that were rendered, the family therapist can take reasonable public actions that will reveal that the client received treatment, e.g., by turning the delinquent account over to a collection agency. Similarly, if a client has filed a charge, say before an ethics committee of a professional organization, the family therapist has a right to clear the record, even if the charge is later withdrawn.

Without the right to protect his or her professional reputation, the practitioner is rendered impotent in the face of a vindictive or pathological client. For example, if a delusional client's pathology leads him or her to believe that there has been sexual intercourse with the therapist and to file a complaint, the family therapist must be authorized to aggressively clear his or her reputation, such as by offering personality test data about the client to the ethics review committee. Even with such defensive efforts, the professional is apt to suffer unjustified consequences to his or her reputation. Unfortunately, there is little else that can be done—except in those instances where the family therapist can construct a bona fide legal (tort) action against the client; but to do so would require, among other legal criteria, that the client knowingly acted without a reasonable basis for a legal action (and many courts are reluctant to accept such a countersuit).

THE STANDARD OF CARE

Establishing a standard of care for covering sexual matters in family therapy can be a difficult challenge. To promote practical notions that will provide safeguards, let us consider the general legal requirements for the standard of care and how they apply to family therapy.

In practical terms, the standard of care refers to the quality of services that the client can justly expect from the family therapist. But there is a legal meaning as well. In legal terms, the standard of care refers to the family therapist's fulfilling his or her *duty* of care to the client. The emphasis upon the word "duty" comes from the fact that legal sanctions may be brought against the therapist when there is a failure to fulfill the standard of care. Stated differently, a breach of the standard of care makes it possible for the client to obtain a remedy through court action.

For the conscientious family therapist, one of the most perplexing problems is that there is no fixed standard of care. There must be a blend of idiosyncratic factors (such as the application of the legal "subjective test," i.e., the circumstances of the particular situation) and nomothetic factors (such as the application of the legal "objective test," i.e., what the reasonable client could expect of the typical therapist). While there is a blend, the controlling test is usually the objective one; that is, the standard of care derives from what a like professional would do in a like set of circumstances. There are exceptions, as will be discussed shortly.

One of the first steps in defining the standard of care is to understand the criterion of the "reasonable person." Again, there is no specific definition—the "reasonable person" is a mythical conglomeration of characteristics and expectations.

For the client, there must be a reasonable expectation. If the client is disappointed by the fact that the family therapist has not performed some miracle cure, there is no breach of the standard of care—unless, of course, the family therapist has foolishly given guarantees of miraculous cures or contracted to produce a therapeutic result that was unattainable. But if the client expects the family therapist to exercise reasonable precautions or professional ethics and the family therapist does not do so (say by taking advantage of transference reactions for his or her own sexual gratification), there was a reasonable expectation and it has been violated—and there is cause for legal action.

Also for the client, there is a legal prescription that the family therapist must consider the client's particular problems. That is, if a client has special vulnerabilities, be they psychological or physical, and the family therapist knows or should have known about them, a failure to properly accommodate these unique needs can result in a breach of the standard of care. For example, leading the client into an affective exploration of a highly charged sexual area, say incest, knowing (or supposedly knowing) that the client had weak ego controls and the potential of suffering emotional devastation, and then not handling the evoked affect to the benefit of the client, could result in the family therapist's failing to meet the standard of care.

Note that there need not be a superior level of service. All that is required on the part of the family therapist is the possession and exercise of knowledge and skill common to a member of the profession in good standing (Prosser, 1971). It should also be noted, however, that if advancement of knowledge, skill, or practice were available to the professional for a minimal expenditure of money or energy, the entire discipline or profession might be found to be in violation of the standard of care. For example, it might be a feeble, ineffective defense to assert that "no family therapist in this area does a formal diagnostic assessment of every client seen for sex therapy," if, in fact, such a personality screening could be done with limited expenditure (such as by administering the Minnesota Multiphasic Personality Inventory to all clients) as a way of warding off the occurrence of situations that could produce extreme effects for the client, such as the example of emotional flooding alluded to earlier.

In the past (and still to this day to a large extent), the determination of the standard of care relied heavily upon what similar professionals did in the immediate geographical area. Thus, if no family therapist in a particular city did diagnostics before doing sex therapy, that would determine the standard of care that had to be fulfilled. But there is a trend away from such parochialism. Today more and more recognition is being given to national practices and standards. Local standards are still seen as highly relevant, but they need not be all-determining.

This broader framework is especially applicable when the service being provided reflects a specialization. For family therapy, there has long been a mixture of "strange bedfellows"; the amount of academic training has varied from little or no college to extensive postdoctoral studies, and yet all can be labeled "family therapists." It would not be unexpected, therefore, for one family therapist, say a minister with Bible college training, to assert that he or she should not be held to the same standard of care as, say, a clinical psychologist with a Ph.D. degree—even though both advertise themselves in the telephone directory's yellow pages as family therapists.

Legal consideration is given to a particular therapist's training. A minister would not typically be expected to always meet the standards expected of a clinical psychologist. On the other hand, if the client were led to believe, in a reasonable fashion, that the minister was providing the same treatment as could be received from a clinical psychologist, the same standard of care might well be applied.

In this age of certification programs in marriage, family, and sex therapy emanating from national professional organizations, the possible distinctions between levels of training or disciplines become even more obscure. For example, most attorneys would probably give careful thought to arguing that there is a single standard of care for all professionals who achieve "Clinical Member" status in the American Association for Marriage and Family Therapy (AAMFT), even though one might be a minister and another a clinical psychologist. Of course, the certification boards, such as within AAMFT, maintain (presumably) the same standards when acting upon credentials, but inevitably the substantive differences in training will result in variations in knowledge, skill, and practice.

Incidentally, the same consideration stated for national organizations applies to state statutory licensing and certification programs. For example, being licensed as a marriage and family counselor by the state automatically connotes to the public that a standard of care has been attained, and asserting training distinctions (again, say between a minister and a clinical psychologist) would be hard to defend in a courtroom.

Family therapists are also prone to think that their individual theoretical approach justifies certain practices. To a very limited degree that may be true, but the preponderance of weight will be placed on how adequate the theoretical school is in meeting the more general standard of care. Prosser (1971) points out that any theoretical approach "must be the line of thought of at least a respectable minority of the profession" (p. 163). Glenn (1974) believes that legal evaluations of the theoretical approach will be based on a comparison with the closest other theoretical approach, which will, of course, often be a rather traditional model.

It would seem that apostles of an experimental or nontraditional approach to family therapy are assuming a clear-cut risk of facing a legal action with a minimum, at best, of professional support. It is not enough to proceed with the notion that stating "Well, systems theory says . . ." or "We gestaltists believe . . ." (or whatever the advocated theory might be) will provide an exemption from being compared with other theoretical schools and other practitioners who might be prone to condemn the experimental nontraditional approach.

When dealing with sexual issues in family therapy, it is certainly prudent to proceed with the frame of reference that a broader than usual comparative analysis will be applied in any ensuing legal action. That is, the emotional, taboo atmosphere that still prevails for sex therapy (Szasz, 1980) supports the observation that any legal challenge to a professional practice will draw from diverse theories, and the justification for sex therapy will have to be better formulated than the justification for some less emotional area, such as career planning, child development, and so on.

To avoid violating the prevailing standard of care, the family therapist involved in treating sexual matters should: (1) strive to stay abreast of research and authoritative positions on sex in therapy; (2) be open to conforming to the standards and guidelines promulgated by professional organizations (being certified as a sex therapist or as a marriage and family therapist is a distinct aid in defending one's professional actions); and (3) seek a supervisory relationship with a professional (even if it is with a colleague/peer) who will be informed about how the therapy is proceeding (having someone else available to attest "Yes, I knew that was what was happening and it seemed like the right thing to do in that case" is an excellent legal defense). Also keeping clients fully informed as to what to expect in sex therapy and assuring them that they have the choice regarding certain ideas or behaviors constitutes the essential legal protection of "informed consent" (Woody, in press). Finally, a written set of standards made available to every client is documentation of what could be reasonably expected and that informed consent has been given.

DUTY TO WARN

A number of court cases have held that the psychotherapist, notwithstanding the revered concepts of confidentiality and privileged communication, must be prepared to warn others if a client can be expected to inflict harm upon them. Most notably, *Tarasoff v. Regents of University of California**
made it quite clear that legal liability will attach to the therapist who knows of intended harm and does not take action to prevent it, such as by warning the intended victim. The court stated: ". . . when a psychotherapist determines or pursuant to the standards of his profession should determine, that his patient presents a serious danger of violence to another he incurs an obligation to use reasonable care to protect the intended victim against such danger . . ." (p. 425). The family therapist is no exception to this legal rule.

Sexual matters create special problems. There is no doubt that predicting violence in the broad sense is difficult enough, but to predict sexual harm to another is even more difficult. Yet legal liability can be incurred if the family

---

*17 Cal. 3d 425, 551 P.2d 334 (Cal. Sup. Ct. 1976).

therapist does not reasonably take action to prevent sexual harm—before it occurs!

Consider the following situation. A 35-year-old, unmarried male comes for an initial appointment. The patient states openly that he lives alone, has few friends, seldom leaves his apartment, and is obsessed with thoughts of physically and sexually assaulting young boys. He admits that he has repeatedly exposed his genitals to children (by dropping his pants at playgrounds and then fleeing the area), and says that whenever he is at a park or playground (which he often visits), "I constantly think about sticking things in the ass-holes of the little boys." He reveals a long psychiatric record, but is no longer receiving treatment. After this information, he indicates that he came for this session because he is scheduled to take the 12-year-old son of a family friend on a European vacation and he fears that he will sexually molest him "when I have him alone so far from home."

Needless to say, there are many signs of danger to the child—the client is literally crying out for someone to take action to prevent his going on the trip with the boy. Yet when told of the jeopardy he is entering into, he vehemently asserts (throughout several subsequent sessions) that he will "just control myself," "rent two rooms," and "try to treat him as a son." In other words, he resists canceling the trip and does not seem to be coming up with any valid safeguards against harmful impulses.

Is there a legal duty to warn? Probably so. What can be done? That is the problem!

In this case, the client refused to identify the child by name, thereby foreclosing the possibility of notifying the parents. Other options would include: (1) petitioning the mental health board for involuntary commitment (but in this case, involuntary commitment required *both* a danger to self or others *and* insanity, and it was unlikely that the client would be adjudged insane); (2) contacting the state's children's protective services, authorized by statute to intervene in child abuse cases (and when this was attempted, the response was "Well, there is nothing we can do because no abuse has occurred yet, but we're willing to offer the man counseling—which, of course, he was already receiving); (3) continuing to see the client for therapy, in hopes that he would (in the four weeks before the long-scheduled trip) gain insight into the risk to both himself and the boy and cancel his plans, and/or achieve therapeutic change to the degree that it could confidently be predicted that he would control any harmful impulses (which, given his chronic psychiatric history, seemed unlikely); or (4) doing nothing and risking the harm that could occur to the child and the possibility that his parents would bring suit for the therapist's failing to fulfill the duty to warn.

It should be noted that, since the state statute offered immunity from legal action to persons who referred a case to the children's protective service involving abuse that "had occurred or was occurring," there was no statutory protection against legal action for an error in predicting possible future abuse. Granted, it might be expected that the courts would strain to justify (and would probably find in favor of) the professional who exercised his or her duty to warn in a reasonable manner (certainly there were enough warning signs in this case to support the thesis that predicting harm to the child was reasonable), but the point remains that a legal action for violating the privileged communication of a therapeutic relationship could feasibly occur.

As this case turned out, the client recognized the risk to himself and the child and canceled the trip; he also entered a day-care treatment program at a psychiatric facility. The case exemplifies, however, the fact that the therapist may well encounter a sexual situation requiring professional action that will have to be taken without any protective legal cloak—it will be individual integrity and good faith motivating the professional into action for the welfare of another person or society.

There will be situations where any claim to privileged communication or the right to privacy will be negated by the client, and in that case the family therapist is legally protected in taking action. Consider the following situation. Child neglect charges have resulted in a husband and wife and their three young children coming for family therapy. During the sessions, it emerges that the parents have engaged in incest and, along with another family, have photographed the children performing sexual activities. No one knows about the sexual abuse except the family therapist, and it goes without saying that the adults do not want it revealed.

While there is no duty to report past abuse, unless it is apt to occur again, if the abuse is currently happening, the family therapist could be legally liable if he or she does not take action to eliminate the abuse. In this case, there are several legal protections for the family therapist. Rather than go into all of the legal fine points, suffice it to say that the continuation of the abuse qualifies for a report to the state's children's protective services, with accompanying immunity from legal action (state statutes on remaining anonymous and having immunity from legal action may differ, so familiarity with the law in one's home state is essential). Further, the minute a third party enters into the scene, there is no constitutional right to privacy. In this case, the inclusion of another family in the photographing of the children performing sexually led to any right to privacy being lost—there could be no reasonable expectation of confidentiality. In a similar case, *Lovisi v. Slayton,** involving a couple's advertising for a sexual partner in a "swinger's" magazine, the court stated: "once they accept onlookers, whether they are close friends, chance acquaintances, observed 'peeping Toms' or paying customers, they may not exclude the state as a constitutionally forbidden intruder."

CONCLUSION

By its very nature, family therapy requires dealing with sexual matters. These may relate to childhood psychosexual development, family attitudes about sex, sexual relations between spouses (or with "significant others"), or sexual behaviors that create a disruptive influence intra- or interpersonally or that violate societal and legal restrictions.

Clearly, there is a mandate for the family therapist to have certain diagnostic and therapeutic knowledge and skills that can be enlisted for effective intervention. Moreover, much thought must be given to the numerous ethical and legal considerations that are unique to therapy for sexual issues.

There is a special and highly forceful societal expectation created for the family therapist's dealings with sex. Of all areas addressed in family therapy, sexual issues unquestionably thrust ethical and legal judgments onto the family therapist with an unprecedented impact.

REFERENCES

American Association of Sex Educators, Counselors, and Therapists. *Code of ethics.* Washington, D.C.: AASECT, 1978.

American Psychological Association. Ethical principles of psychologists. *American Psychologist,* 1981, *36,* 633-638.

Arbuckle, D.S. The self of the counselor. *Personnel and Guidance Journal,* 1966, *44,* 807-812.

Arnold, D.L. Working with persons going into counseling. *Counselor Education and Supervision,* 1967, *6,* 171-178.

Glenn, R.D. Standard of care in administering non-traditional psychotherapy. *University of California, Davis Law Review,* 1974, *7,* 56-83.

Masters, W.H., Johnson, V.E., & Kolodny, R.D. (Eds.). *Ethical issues in sex therapy and research.* Boston: Little, Brown, 1977.

---

*539 F.2d 349 (4th Cir. 1976).

Mezzano, J. Self insight of graduate students in guidance. *Counselor Education and Supervision*, 1968, *7*, 397-398.

Prosser, W.L. *Handbook of the law of torts* (4th ed.). St. Paul: West, 1971.

Shoben, E.J., Jr. The counseling experience as personal development. *Personnel and Guidance Journal*, 1965, *44*, 224-230.

Szasz, T. *Sex by prescription*. New York: Anchor Press/Doubleday, 1980.

Woody, R.H. *Psychobehavioral counseling and therapy: Integrating behavioral and insight techniques*. New York: Appleton-Century-Crofts, 1971.

Woody, R.H. Legal dimensions of the human service relationship. In R.H. Woody (Ed.), *Human services law*. San Francisco: Jossey-Bass, in press.

Wright, R.H. What to do until the malpractice lawyer comes: A survivor's manual. *American Psychologist*, 1981, *36*, 12, 1535-1541.

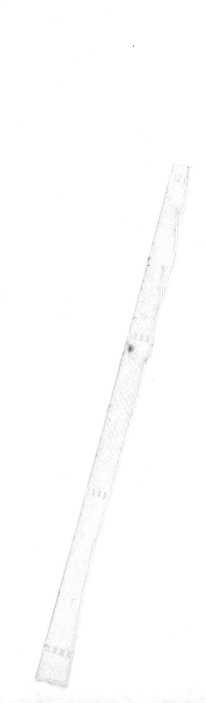